The Lens (

Ov

Every Life Challenge

By: Rani Landa

This book is a personal account of the author's experiences with domestic violence and her journey to finding peace through Christianity. The views and opinions expressed in this book are those of the author and do not necessarily reflect the views of any organisations or entities with which the author is affiliated.

Published in UK, Year 2024

Disclaimer:

The information presented in this book is based on the author's personal experiences and is intended for educational and informational purposes only. The author and publisher make no warranties or representations regarding the accuracy or completeness of the content. Readers are encouraged to seek professional advice and support related to issues of domestic violence or any other topics discussed in this book.

Contents

Dedications

This book is dedicated first of all to the Holy Spirit, whom I met through my faith in Jesus Christ, my Lord and Saviour. It is through the Holy Spirit that I was inspired to write my autobiography.

I also dedicate this book to my husband and every member of my family, who are the reason that this book was written.

I want to dedicate this book to all who are led to read it, in the hope that something shared in this book will inspire you and bring new hope and perspective to your life journey.

"But the Helper, the Holy Spirit, whom the Father will send in My name, He will teach you all things and bring to your remembrance all that I have said to you." **(John 14:26)**

Acknowledgements

My life came to a major turning point after I was invited to Charis Bible College. Andrew Wommack Ministries, Walsall, UK.

My experiences of three and half years in this beacon of light place changed and impacted my life in a very positive, empowering way. Spending five hours a day. Monday to Friday in this environment was a very refreshing and uplifting experience. I am so thankful to the teachers, lecturers and my fellow classmates and friends for being a part of the journey marked out for me. I believe this pathway was from the God of my newfound faith in Jesus Christ. It was a privilege and honour to be taught such great truths, wisdom, and revelations from the bible by men and women with integrity and character who believed and reflected what they taught with such passion.

I am grateful to Andrew and Jamie Wommack, the founders of Charis Bible College. They run these colleges all around the world, impacting people's lives and empowering them in positive, constructive ways. They certainly impacted my life with their teaching on the unconditional love of God. They helped me understand the meaning of the finished work of the Cross of Jesus Christ, the righteousness of God, and much, much more. These three and half years have left a sweet, lasting aroma in the core of my being and has impacted the people around me to this point of my life journey.

About The Author

I was born on August 24th, 1962, in a Sikh family. When I was six months old, my mother and I migrated to England, where I was educated. I am married and blessed with four children and eight grandchildren. My career spans thirty years in the health industry, and I have also owned a Fish and Chips business, which was a pillar of support in the community. This business wasn't just about selling food; it was about providing a listening ear, allowing people to make important phone calls, and ensuring that elderly individuals found their way home safely. Through these acts, I found meaning and purpose in my life.

A pivotal moment in my journey occurred in January 2006 when I experienced what I believe to be the tangible presence of God. This encounter was a turning point. Even though I was taking small steps of faith in my newfound walk with Jesus Christ, there was a deep-rooted peace and assurance after I invited Jesus into my heart as my Lord, Saviour, and friend. This decision brought guidance and inspiration from the Holy Spirit. Despite life's imperfections, I felt a sense of hope that everything would work out.

In November 2006, I took the significant step of water baptism, publicly confessing my faith in Jesus Christ. It was humbling and surprising to hear mature believers see potential in me that I couldn't see at the time. Their words of encouragement uplifted me, affirming that God had great plans for me.

However, my journey wasn't without challenges. Facing spiritual abuse and lack of support in some churches, I decided to seek God's peace and presence in the security of my own home. In 2011, a close friend and sister in Christ invited me to Charis Bible College. Initially hesitant due to past church experiences, I eventually decided to attend. This decision brought relief and joy as I found answers to my questions about my new faith in Jesus Christ. Learning about God's unconditional love was transformative, healing my deep-rooted wounds and insecurities.

Coming from a Sikh background, the teachings about the righteousness of Jesus Christ and His sacrifice on the Cross were profound. They brought incredible peace to my mind and body. I learned that salvation is not based on my actions but on simply believing in Jesus and His righteousness. Hallelujah!

During a time of deep insecurity and fear, taking the step of faith to attend Bible College was transformative. The Jesus living inside me became a magnet, drawing people to Him as I allowed His love to flow through me. I completed three years of training at Charis Bible College, graduating in May 2014. Since then, my network and connections have expanded worldwide, enriching my personal and family relationships.

During my second year of training, as we prepared for a mission trip, I felt God speaking to me through the scripture Hosea 4:6, "My people are destroyed for lack of knowledge." I understood that God brought me to Bible college to learn about His unconditional love so I could share it with the world. My life's mission became to communicate how deeply humans are loved and cared for by Jesus Christ, who gave His life to bring us back to Himself.

Throughout my life, I have held various jobs, from packaging and sewing to pedestrian patrol for children. Each experience has shaped me and prepared me for the purpose God has designed for my life.

Introduction

This captivating book is the true story of a courageous woman who defied all odds to carve her own path. Born into a family steeped in tradition that expected her to marry early, she endured an abusive marriage that she persevered through. In her autobiography, she handles all, from the difficulties she faced with cultural expectations to the challenges she faced in an unhealthy relationship.

However, this book is not just a chronicle of suffering. It is a powerful message of resilience and finding a better path. Through her untiring spirit and newfound faith, she transformed her pain into strength and emerged victorious.

As you read through the pages, you'll witness a remarkable transformation - a woman discovering her inner strength and purpose, perceiving the world with a fresh perspective.

This book is a roadmap to living a life of triumph, filled with lessons of discipline, focus, and perseverance, showing us how to face our battles and emerge victorious. The chapters ahead will take readers on a journey of hope, resilience, and the indomitable power of the human spirit to overcome even the darkest times.

Introduction

Chapter 1
Early Life & Upbringing

"There are many plans in a man's heart, Nevertheless the LORD's counsel—that will stand."

- Proverbs 19:21 NKJV

Before I start telling my life story, I'll begin by sharing it was an extraordinary journey, filled with both highs and lows that most of us encounter in life. In this book, I hope to share my journey, including moments of hope and moments of despair. But it's also a story of resilience and determination that can serve as a beacon of hope during the darkest days of one's life. A reminder that even amid adversity, there is always hope. Throughout my journey, I have learned that hope does not disappoint. Reading this life story will awaken and encourage others to know that there is a truth that can set us free when we pursue it.

As you move through the chapters of this book, I'll be sharing experiences that have played a part in shaping who I am today. Memories of my upbringing and the discipline I learned during my early years have remained with me and shaped my future. In this chapter, I'll reveal some defining moments of my life and the obstacles I had to overcome to reach where I am today. Despite the challenges, I always held onto a sense of hope from within, telling me that it would get better.

As I reminisce about my childhood, I am taken back to the world bursting with vibrant colours and enchanting tales. Born into a Sikh household, I was surrounded by the echoes of ancient traditions and religious customs that infused every aspect of our daily lives.

Being a girl in such a household meant that academic pursuits were not a priority. Instead, we were expected to focus on domestic duties such as cooking, cleaning, and learning the art of homemaking. While our male counterparts were encouraged to pursue academic excellence, we were always being taught and pushed to do better in the household chores without realising that it was a training ground to become a good wife and mother someday.

Most of my days were spent in daily household chores and helping my mother look after my siblings. Although the world outside my bedroom window looked very attractive, I had no desire to be a part of it. I felt a sense of security just being enclosed within my environment.

The only glimpses I had of life beyond our doorstep were through the flickering light of oil lamps during power cuts and through the stories told by visiting relatives. However, as I look back on those days, I realise how much those traditions shaped my life.

Despite the warmth and comfort of my upbringing, as I reflect on my past, I can't help but ask myself the question: "What if?" What if I had pursued my education and chased my dreams? What if I had followed a different path, one that didn't lead to marriage and domesticity? The norms that once felt like a warm embrace now seem like chains holding back the potential of every girl's heart.

My mother played an essential role in shaping my life, leaving an indelible mark on my personality that has kept me strong to this day. Her grace and elegance were unmatched, and her family background was one of prestige and honour. Her marriage to my father was arranged, and my father cherished having her beside him.

She was the backbone of our family and held our lives together with her capable hands. However, at times, her love for us would be overbearing and challenging, causing us to feel trapped in her desire for us to be perfect in every possible way. Being the oldest and the firstborn of the family, I bore the brunt of my mum's high expectations.

At times, I felt like I was walking on eggshells, always trying to please my mother. She kept a persistent eye on all of us and knew just what to say to keep us in line. Although she could display a stern and fierce character, there was also a gentle, caring, and loving side to her that would come out at times. This softer side of her character would melt away all the anguish within us.

Her love was like a gentle breeze guiding us through life's fields, but at times, it could be like a sudden storm leaving us feeling breathless and a little bruised. As the oldest child, a lot more was expected of me. From feeding the youngest to settling disputes between siblings, my days were never short of things to do.

The pressure was always there to walk a tightrope between responsibility and childhood, knowing that even the slightest mistake would lead to some kind of discipline or correction. Sadly, my mother passed away at the early age of 59.

The memories of my childhood are etched in my mind like a vivid painting, and as time goes by, they remain ever-present. However, the feelings and emotions that were once attached to those memories have gradually melted away with the passing years. As I continue to grow in my newfound faith in Jesus Christ, I have come to realise that those feelings and emotions cannot hold me back from the life of freedom and liberty that I have found in my new faith.

I recall those times when my parents would leave us home alone and put us in charge. Those were moments of pure joy and unbridled laughter, like stolen sweets. My siblings and I would run around the house, our voices echoing through the empty rooms as we chased each other and found new places to hide. But we always knew that our fun would be short-lived, and we would freeze at the exact moment before our parents returned.

In retrospect, it's a memory that brings a bittersweet smile to my face, as it reminds me of the complex dance of love and control that played out under our roof. My mother's influence, though sometimes heavy-handed, shaped me in ways I wouldn't have imagined. Her high standards and expectations were always present, and it was challenging to meet them at times. However, it also pushed us to be better.

Her influence echoed in my own marriage, impacting the way I strived for perfection in the fear of disappointing the ones I loved. It was a lesson that I carried with me throughout my life, one that taught me to be resilient determined, and always strive for excellence in everything I did.

My Sikh Marriage At 16 Years Old

When I was just sixteen years old, my life took a dramatic turn that altered its course forever. In accordance with the customs of our culture, my parents began the search for a suitable match for me. Their approach to matchmaking was simple yet effective, relying on subtle glances and the exchange of tokens to communicate volumes. Before long, a match was found, and he, along with his family, was invited to our house. It was an exciting time for all of us as we prepared to receive them.

Asian Sikh functions usually require women to dress in traditional attire consisting of shalwar, kameez, and chunni, which is a combination of pants, a top, and a scarf. In the Sikh community, there is a customary separation of men and women, with them sitting in separate rooms. When they came to visit me and meet my family, the men sat in the front lounge while the women sat in the back lounge next to the kitchen. There were three women and three men who came to see me and meet the family.

As per custom, we made them feel very welcome by serving tea, Asian sweets, and savouries. Then, it was time for me to make an entrance. As I walked into the room, my heart raced like never before, and I kept my eyes down as I looked at the floor. The room went completely silent for a moment.

My future mother-in-law looked up at me with kindness reflecting in her eyes and asked me my name. Her gentle demeanour immediately put me at ease. I gently replied my name is Rani. There were no prying questions, no judgmental glances, just a gentle inspection to see how I looked and a silent exchange of smiles that spoke volumes.

Among the men was my future father-in-law, seemingly kind and polite with a mischievous glint in his eyes. A similar thing was taking place in the front lounge – my father, brothers, and other family members were getting to know my future husband in the same way.

And then came the sweet dance of acceptance - the clinking of coins, the rustle of sugar, and a whispered promise that hung in the air. The moment was nothing short of magical, filling me with a sense of hope for a bright and happy future.

Although my life until that point had been far from miserable, it had been challenging. At such a young age, being taught and given responsibilities was beyond my comprehension. Despite all this, I had a feeling of hope and excitement that as I entered the next chapter of my life, I would be seen and accepted in a new way.

Bride-To-Be

The moment I got engaged, my life took an unexpected turn. It felt as if I had shed my old skin and had emerged as a new, transformed person – a bride-to-be on a journey to a new chapter of my life. The wedding preparations were all swept up in a whirlwind of excitement, anticipation, and joy.

As the big day approached, our house became a hub of activity. Relatives and friends wanted to extend their support. Every now and then, they would come and take part in the preparation. I felt loved, supported, and anxious at the same time.

On the day of the wedding, everything looked perfect in every way. The vibrant colours of tradition were everywhere from the intricate-silk fabrics that whispered secrets of love to the intricate folds that symbolised forever. I felt very special and was the centre of attention, enjoying every passing moment.

The ancient rituals soothed my anxieties, replacing them with a gentle hum of anticipation. The air was filled with laughter and blessings, a symphony of joy orchestrated by the hands of fate. It was a day I would never forget – a moment frozen in time, a canvas painted with the colours of love and happiness.

As I reflect on the past and think about my arranged marriage, I remember not even considering who my husband was. I had never met him beforehand and knew nothing about him. However, as the idea of my wedding day began to take shape in my mind, I found myself filled with a sense of excitement and adventure. The very thought of all the beautiful attire that I would get to wear felt very appealing and attractive. I felt overwhelmed with joy when guests began to arrive with beautiful gifts, coconuts, sugar, and money.

The day I had always longed for finally arrived, and it was nothing short of magical. The wedding ceremony spanned three days, each moment filled with age-old traditions and customs that were deeply ingrained in our culture.

Looking back now, I realise perhaps my feelings and emotions came from a young teenager dreaming of a happy forever ending. Although the concept of an arranged marriage was not new to me, I couldn't help but feel grateful for this sense of belonging and continuity that it brought to my life. It was an extraordinary time of jubilation and festivity that I will always cherish in my heart.

The days immediately following my wedding days were nothing short of a beautiful dream. Everything was new and thrilling, and I was filled with a sense of adventure and anticipation. My in-laws seemed warm, kind, and welcoming.

However, as time passed by, I began to see the darker side of my new life, which will be unfolded in the coming chapters of this book. The harsh realities of marriage and family life slowly began to reveal themselves. Back then, I had no idea that my journey was going to be much more complicated and challenging than I had ever imagined.

Chapter 2
Understanding & Overcoming Cultural Constraints

"But we have this treasure in earthen vessels that the excellence of the power may be of God and not of us. We are hard-pressed on every side, yet not crushed; we are perplexed, but not in despair; persecuted, but not forsaken; struck down, but not destroyed".

II Corinthians 4:7-9 NKJV

"What will people say?"

As I replay the events of my life, this particular phrase has always been a guiding principle for me. Not just me, for that matter. It has played a crucial role in the life of every other woman from traditional Asian Indian culture.

I was only a child since when this question started overshadowing me. It would echo in my mind every time I made a decision or chose a path for myself. Growing up, I was told that if I do something bad, it won't just tarnish my reputation. It would put my family's honour at stake too. Hence, I was responsible for protecting my family's reputation too and I carried this weight everywhere I went, every move I made. For me, decisions were never casual choices. Rather, they were scales that were constantly weight to gauge the impact they might have on my family's honour.

It's hard enough to live up to your family's expectations and I was asked to fulfil the expectations of the community I lived in. The set standards set by society were inflexible and I was supposed to steer my own and dreams and desires while ensuring I meet those standards. Oh, and saying no? That wasn't an option ever. I wasn't

8

even allowed to question anything. As long as I was meeting the societal standards, I was good to go – even if it meant sacrificing some of my own goals and aspirations.

Now that I look back, I see that this immense pressure to abide by the rules society set for us wasn't something I had chosen for myself. This heavy cloak of honour was wrapped around me by our culture and it was made sure that I never took it off by linking it with my father and family name's dignity. As a daughter, I constantly had the responsibility to uphold my family's reputation.

And let me tell you, this responsibility was no joke. From a very young age, we were taught that if we are ever faced with a choice between saving our life and protecting our family's name from even a bit of tarnish, we should put our family's reputation first. It's this burden we carry everywhere and it shapes our very existence.

Consider it more like an invisible power that guides every choice we make. We tread carefully when making decisions in life, even if it means we have to give up our own wishes or goals. For me, this force was my family's reputation. It guided me through the complex rules of society and influenced the choices I made, sometimes even making me forget my own dreams.

If I'm being honest, personal aspirations were never at the front seat in my life. My basic needs, fundamental concerns that should have been a priority, were often neglected and ignored. My education is perhaps the biggest example of this. Learning was never an easy job for me. It was a constant battle that made me feel like I'm up to no good. I was always lagging behind my classmates since it was hard for me to grasp new concepts quickly, and it left me feeling frustrated.

Unfortunately, my family never understood how difficult it was for me to study. Besides, they were never in favour of educating girls, so they didn't even try comprehend the struggles I was going through.

I felt like I was constantly fighting an uphill battle, trying to match the pace of my peers while also meeting the expectations of my family and society. My entire life was divided into two worlds, with my personal aspirations on one side and the responsibilities of my home on another.

Dyslexia

Only I knew the struggles I faced whenever I tried to read from a textbook. I would try to focus on the written text but the letters would look like they are moving, creating a maze that I could never make sense of. For years, I used to believe that I face this challenge because I don't try hard enough. Eventually, though, I discovered I have a learning disability called dyslexia.

Although I was never diagnosed, I eventually learned about my challenges. I got to know that children like me can easily reach their full potential if they are given the right attention and support. But only if I was that fortunate. My family never understood, let alone support, my learning journey and being dyslexic limited my accomplishments. Much of that time, I did not even think about my struggles because I wasn't even aware of my condition.

Moreover, in my society, a girl's ultimate destiny is marriage. It was just the way things were supposed to be, or so I thought. But now I think that if I had received the support and understanding I needed, I could have achieved so much more. But at the time, I didn't know any different. I simply accepted my struggles as a part of life and focused on the expectations set by society. It wasn't until later that I realised how much I had missed out on.

As I think about it now, it surprises me to notice how my upbringing had deeply embedded these cultural values in me. The elders believed if a woman is not married at a young age, she might make hasty decisions about love. Believe me, this wasn't just a notion – it was a perception. But wait, there's more to that. It was incredibly important to protect a girl's virginity as it was not just about personal honour. As I said before, her entire family's prestige was associated with it.

Now you'd think it would stop there. Well, it did not. The society I lived in had come up with protective measures like early marriage or limited social interactions to prevent women from falling into a ditch.

Wedding off their daughters at a fairly young age was just a reflection of this mindset. Mind you, it wasn't only about finding a good match for the couple. Instead, it was also about checking if their families were compatible. They believed that growing up together would allow the couple to understand and love each other more deeply. It doesn't make much sense right now, but it surely did back in the day.

Besides, these values were so deep-rooted that one could not dare question them. It wasn't until I started doubting these beliefs that I realised how much they had influenced my life. All my life, I had been blindly abiding by these unsaid rules and it led me down a certain path. A path that almost always didn't align with my own desires.

The Sikh Wedding

I was born a Sikh and in my culture, marriage was way more than a romantic meeting between two dreamy souls. It is more like a collaboration between two families, each bringing something to the table. Unlike what we see in the West, this union doesn't just represent the 'I do' affair. It celebrates a sacred and lifelong commitment. It is a considered a cosmic journey with its fair share of emotional, spiritual, and physical aspects.

My elders taught me that marriage is not just a partnership; it is a special bond that requires commitment and selflessness. A bond that prioritises your partner's needs over your own. Even though my marriage didn't exactly take the conventional route, these lessons were always there in the back of my mind.

Sikh culture is mostly knowns for its bright weddings and unique traditions. But today, let me tell you something. Beneath all that glamour and glitz that you see, the families are actually struggling with challenges to make the expenses meet. And no, you can't wed off your son or daughter in a restricted budget, because if the guests are not happy, your event will be marked unsuccessful.

In Sikh weddings, particularly, keeping the guests in high spirits is perhaps even more important than the couple riding off into the sunset. The post-celebration should be huge, no ifs and buts.

The marriages themselves are rich with unique traditions. In Sikhism, both families meet at the bride's house before the grand day. Traditionally, the couple isn't even allowed to glance at each other until the wedding day, but nowadays, I've seen it happen. Once the potential bride and groom are considered a good match, the parents turn into event planners, and they begin coordinating everything from setting the date to finalising the guest list.

The engagement ceremony is called "shagan" and it's the final yes from both sides of the family. The groom is given Laddu (an Indian sweet) with blessings – marking a sweet start to the marriage. After the ceremony ends, the groom is officially marked reserved. And then, it's time for the next move.

As part of the same ceremony, the groom's family sends gifts for the bride. I was walking on air the day I received a bounty of dried fruits, sweets, a beautiful chunni (scarf), and a jewellery set. I was then dolled up for the event with all the accessories my in-laws had brought for me.

The actual wedding day is considered the grand finale. Mine took place at the Sikh temple, and it was centred around the Guru Granth Sahib. We walked around it four times while the Giani sang holy hymns that made it all felt surreal.

Apart from simply following traditions, the time before my weddings was filled with love and happiness. Every event was a special moment for me that I've kept safe in a memory book full of cultural traditions and most importantly, love that surpassed the traditions.

In my society, weddings are portrayed no less than a fairy tale. Like many others, I also believed it to be true until it was my turn to experience it. As I already mentioned in the previous chapter, there was an air of excitement when my wedding was arranged. It's rare to be the centre of attention in households like mine, almost like finding a needle in a haystack. Even on days when you're sick, you can't get the attention from your family. So, when I found myself surrounded by love, attention and presents from all directions, it was all quite overwhelming.

I had been to the weddings of countless family members, so I knew how excited and overjoyed the brides are. I couldn't help but feel envious of the attention they used to get, even before fully understanding what marriage was all about. But, soon after the wedding, I began to realise that it wasn't just about attention and presents. It was about committing to spend the rest of my life with someone, even when it seems impossible.

What we were shown was just one side of the coin—the shining side that filled us with hope and excitement. However, we were kept in darkness from the opposite side of this portrayal. Sometimes I even question myself if that flip side was truly concealed from us? Or, were we too accustomed to it and thought it was ordinary?

We were never informed about the weight of expectations, social pressures, and the need for constant adjustments once we start our married life. It felt like being handed a script, and we performed our roles without ever questioning or looking beyond the stage. Personally, I never found myself questioning this structure of our society because I never thought anything was wrong in it.

Growing up, I saw how my mother took full responsibility of our home and subconsciously, I accepted that this is how my married life would look like as well. After all, it wasn't just my mother's example that I had witnessed. All my cousins led a similar life, so I always assumed that I was also meant to follow the play written for me without ever deviating from it.

Besides, marriage looked like a path to freedom for me – it offered an escape from household responsibilities that overwhelmed me at that young age. I usually accepted life's twists and turns without retaliating. Yet, at times, the dissatisfaction brewing within me would become too much to ignore. It would trigger questions that were far beyond my comprehension. Why was I never given the right to get education? Why couldn't my husband and I find common ground to work through our differences? These unanswered questions kept bothering me, haunting my thoughts long after I had distanced myself from that chaotic past. This continued until I found peace in my new faith in Jesus.

Chapter 3
Educational Life

"Wisdom is the principal thing; Therefore get wisdom. And in all your getting, get understanding. Exalt her, and she will promote you; She will bring you honour, when you embrace her. She will place on your head an ornament of grace; a crown of glory she will deliver to you."

Proverbs 4:7-9 NKJV

Education is everyone's fundamental right, isn't that so? The world we live in now, we take it for granted that every child deserves to go to school and learn. We are challenged with all kinds of emotions when we see an underage child being exploited for labour instead of being educated. We believe that education is the key to a better future.

But what if I told you that this was not always the case? What if I told you that there was a time when education was not a priority in some cultures like mine or even a possibility for many children? What if I told you that I was one of those children?

I grew up in an environment where education was not valued or encouraged for young girls like me. My parents limited mind set was that education was for the boys because they would be the providers of their household. Back then, the prevailing mindset didn't view the absence of education for girls as a major concern, and understandably, it would more than likely get tongues wagging.

But there was a problem. I had a learning disability that made it hard for me to read and write. I had dyslexia, a condition that affects the way the brain processes written information. Words and letters would get jumbled up in my head, and I would struggle to make sense

15

of them. I used to mix up sounds and spellings, and I couldn't even remember what I had just read. This used to be an extremely frustrating and embarrassing experience for me, making me lose confidence in myself.

As I've hinted before in the previous chapters, my educational hurdles were never recognised in my home. I was treated like just another child. You know how some children are different than others? The ones that are not academically as sharp as their siblings? I was considered like one of them. It didn't cross anyone's mind that I might be dealing with issues of my own. Perhaps I'm also to be blamed for a part of it because I never voiced my concerns either. I mean, how could I? Even I didn't know about my condition. I was only five when I was enrolled into a school.

This marked the beginning of a long and painful journey. A journey that challenged my spirit and tested my will to learn. A journey that exposed me to the harsh truths of life and the cruel biases of my society.

However, it was also a journey that moulded me into the person I am today. This is my story. A story of how I turned my life around by converting my struggles into my strengths. A story of how I ended up achieving my dreams.

But before I tell you how I got here, it's important I tell you about how it all began in the first place. Let me take you to the school where I faced my first battles and where I met my first friends. Let me take you to the moments that marked my life, the ones that made me laugh and cry, the ones that broke me and the ones that healed me.

As I remember my early school days, I recall snippets of memories from infant school. It feels like these moments are frozen in time. At that age, the concept of 'learning' was wrapped in the joy of singing rhymes, the thrill of colouring sketchbooks, and the excitement of physical education activities. For a five-year-old, it was all about having fun. Even the perceptive eyes of teachers struggled to discern any learning disabilities in those early vital years of learning.

Little did I know, these carefree days were merely the calm before the storm. The innocence of my early education would soon face the turbulence of dyslexia, altering the course of my educational journey. However, before I start telling you about the challenges that awaited me, let me first guide you through the sunlit corridors of my initial days at infant school, for it wasn't all a tale of adversity, as I've hinted before.

I was born in a conservative family. A family where you were not supposed to step out of the house unnecessarily. And don't even get me started on talking to strangers – it was something strictly forbidden. So, when I stepped into the world of education, I was confused and nervous. The prospect of attending school was new to me and the thought of interacting with hundreds of new faces sent shivers down my spine. And why would it not? A sheltered existence was all I knew so the very idea of stepping out and talking to strangers seemed impossible for me.

I remember standing in front of the school's gate on my first day. As soon as the doors were opened and I stepped inside, I was greeted with hundreds of unfamiliar faces of teachers and students. This introduction to the outside world was overwhelming for me and I couldn't help but long for the familiar comfort of my own home. Usually, the first day of school is a big step for every child. However, for me, it was a giant leap into uncharted territory.

People believe the role your first teacher plays sets the tone for your entire educational journey. It's a notion many people agree with. But if you ask me, I'm not so sure about it. A part of me thinks it's true, but the other part of me tends to disagree. Let me tell you why. I met Mrs Clifton in infant school, my first teacher. She was no less than a beacon of light for me in those early days of schooling. And really, it wasn't just about the academics. I grew so accustomed to her so quickly that she became my comfort zone.

Her bright and radiant face became my guiding star and I would trail behind her in class, seeking constant reassurance.

Even though her accent was unfamiliar, perhaps Irish or Scottish, her words brought comfort and warmth that I couldn't find elsewhere. I don't know how to describe it, it's just she was a source of solace for me.

Come to think of it, it's fascinating how you remember certain moments so clearly, even after so much time has passed. Take Mrs Clifton, for example. I never met her after infant school, but she left an permanent mark in my life. She wasn't just a teacher, she was my home in an entirely foreign environment. Her presence and influence were two factors that shaped my initial learning experience. In fact, it also impacted how I perceived my educational journey – even if it didn't last long.

Infant school continued and as time went on, I gradually got used to the new routine and even made some great friends. The rhymes that initially felt like mere melodies became familiar too, and became a huge part of my early school memories.

The school I attended was quite good at mixing extracurricular activities with learning, and our Annual Sports Day was among the many highlights. I always looked forward to it, as did all my peers.

The Sports Day was all set to be held towards the end of school year, and I couldn't help but feel excited about it. Everyone would start talking about it and preparing for it months in advance, making everyone eager. For a child like me, someone who didn't enjoy learning, Sports Day felt like a break from all of that. It was just pure fun!

With the event drawing nearer, the school turned into a hub of activity. It became a ritual to stay after school for practice as preparations were in full swing. While I may not remember my time in participating the practice races and activities, I do remember the joy of skipping classes for practice. In those moments, it felt like I was no longer buried under the weight of textbooks.

After what felt like an eternity, the day finally arrived. The school on the big field in the school, and the invitations were sent out to parents and teachers alike, making it a major celebration.

Walking into the ground, my heart started beating faster as I saw the sea of faces in the audience. For someone born an introvert, the idea of performing in such a crowd was scary to say the least. However, my heart suddenly swelled with warmth when I walked past the section my family was seated. I saw them cheering for me. At that moment, I was filled with satisfaction and confidence and I no longer felt as nervous as I did when I first stepped onto the ground.

As the day went on, the moment we had all been waiting for arrived – the beginning of races and activities, one after another. The air was filled with excitement, and the combined energy of students and parents created an atmosphere of celebration.

Just when we thought the day was winding down, the principal took hold of the microphone. He made a shocking announcement, revealing a surprise none of us had expected– a final race, but not for the students, for the parents. The announcement sent a ripple of excitement through the crowd and the audience began encouraging the brave parents to step onto the ground to participate in the competition.

I glanced at my family, hoping they might also step onto the field so I could cheer them on. Instead, they silently declined, shaking their heads. While I felt a hint of disappointment, I soon realised it wasn't about me. After all, whether they partake in the race or not was their personal preference. Hence, I decided to focus on the brighter side of the day. Their presence at Sports Day mattered more than this. I still cherish the memory of their cheers and support throughout the day.

Soon, I finished infant school and it was time to enter primary school. For me, this transition was significant as it was the beginning of 'actual' education and learning. My life took a dark turn when my learning disability prevented me from grasping the new concepts that my classmates would easily understand. I gave it my best, but I would fail every time making me believe I was fighting for a lost cause. I began losing what little interest I had in academics.

But then, how long could I keep my struggles from my teachers? They have discerning eyes, don't they? It didn't take them much time to recognise that I'm suffering. At first, they tried giving me individual attention, but once they realised what I was going through, they recommended I should enrol in a special learning school.

Now that was another challenge I had to deal with at home. My parents were hesitant strictly opposed the suggestions of my teachers, as they weren't able to understand the school curriculum. According to them, I was perfectly fine so it was unnecessary to send me to another school. Only if they knew or understood the extent of my struggles with dyslexia, they may have been less resistant to the idea.

My school, however, did not give up. The staff kept discussing the importance of this matter with my parents and after a long and intense discussion, a decision was taken. It was decided that me and a few other peers facing similar challenges will report to a new school every morning. But dropping us there won't be our parents' headache. Rather, the school bus would take us there from our regular school.

Hence, the bus started to punctually pick us up from our regular school and drop us back there at the end of the day, ready for our parents to collect us. This new routine became my 'new normal'. I would leave home early in the morning and return around 3:30 PM. In this new school, the faculty was better equipped to handle students with learning disabilities. This continued throughout almost the rest of my time in primary school.

Now that I think about the time I spent in the special needs school, I don't think it helped improve my learning abilities as much. Granted, it gave me the support I needed, but it's not like my hurdles had disappeared. Eventually, I was reintegrated into the regular primary school by my teachers since they thought I was ready. But was I? If you ask me, I most certainly was not.

However, I decided to go with the flow. And how could I not? I was being pressured by my family and school. So, my only option was to adopt the role of a diligent student. I pretended like I understood every concept and lesson. Yet, when the test papers were distributed, I would always be lost. I will constantly look over my shoulder in search of any external assistance.

What I started as a mere act, it soon turned into a survival strategy – allowing me to cope with the unrealistic standards set by my family and school.

Something my father used to say helped me a lot during this time. Whenever our family was in distress, he would utter in a reassuring voice, 'This too shall pass.' At that age, I didn't really know what it meant but somewhere within me, I knew its purpose. It was something to cling to, something that offered hope for better days.

So, I kept repeating this mantra silently, determined that the challenges I'm facing right now will soon fade into the past. And fade it did.

In a few years, primary school became a part of the past and I did manage to pass it with satisfactory grades. Even though, it gave me quite a tough time, I was relieved to learn that it was finally over. But it now time to move onto the next challenge: secondary school. A transition that felt like moving from a frying pan to a fire.

As expected, secondary school wasn't without its difficulties. In fact, the challenges I experienced here were double of what I encountered in primary school. It wasn't just the academic pressure, though. As I was a teenager now, I also had a list of household chores I had to take care of on daily basis. At times, it would become incredibly difficult to juggle the academic and domestic responsibilities at the same time.

From cleaning to cooking, sewing, and taking care of my younger siblings – I had to do it all. It didn't matter if it was before or after school, the chores would be there waiting for me and my siblings Sometimes, we didn't have not even have enough time to finish all our chores.

There were times I would be fully dressed for school, ready to leave, and my family would ask me to take out the ashes and light the fire before I go. And oh – saying 'no' was a luxury I was always deprived of. Actually, some days I even had to stay back home and help my mother out because apparently, school wasn't that important.

Naturally, such circumstances took a toll on my academic progress. But my family never seemed to notice it because as I have said multiple times before, my education was never a priority for them.

On top of all this, my parents themselves were not familiar to the English Language. Not at all. They couldn't read, write, or even speak it properly. This language barrier was a major obstacle in their daily lives. Whether they wanted to write a letter or read a notice, they wanted me and my siblings to become their guiding hand.

While my challenges in secondary school were no less than a nightmare, they were only the tip of the iceberg. I realised these major and minor issues were now a part of my life and I'll have to find out a way to keep going anyhow. Hence, I decided to hide my silent battles from the world. Mind you, I had formed quite a circle of friends in school by now. But it wasn't easy – it came with a cost. I had to fit into their flawlessly and that made me go to extreme lengths at times.

For instance, the school rules required us to follow a certain dress code – a blouse, grey skirts, and a cardigan. While this might not be a big deal to a lot of people, my parents thought otherwise. As per them, the uniform revealed too much of our body, something that wasn't allowed in our faith.

According to them, this 'nudity' is strictly prohibited in our faith. They insisted I should wear pants with my uniform to appear modest. Now since I was a minority at school, it was already hard enough for me to blend in. Could I afford offering another reason why I should be mocked and bullied? Absolutely not.

So, I came up with a ritual of my own. I used to wear pants underneath my skirt when leaving home and would take them off as soon as I reached the school. This way, I managed to adhere with the school's dress code while preserving my modesty in my family's eye. This continued throughout my tenure in secondary school.

As secondary school came to an end, I noticed something about myself. I realised I was more drawn to some subjects like Geography,

Art, and Religious Studies. Upon giving it some thought, I concluded that it's perhaps because these subjects were more engaging and interesting than technical ones. It was easier for me to understand their concepts, which made me feel like a good student.

It was around this time that my father had an idea. Although it was a simple one, it altered the course of my life. He decided that all of us siblings should visit India one by one. Honestly, the thought of going to India did excite me, but it was also a bit scary. I wanted to meet my relatives in India, but the idea of visiting another country without my family made me feel a bit uneasy.

My father felt he was enhancing our lives by sending us to see where our family roots were. He had made up his mind and none of us could question his decision. Hence, I soon accompanied my grandfather and uncle to a flight to India. I was visiting India for the first time in my life and this maiden visit stretched over five months.

As I had spent all my life in the United Kingdom, I couldn't help but notice the differences between the two countries. Whether I talk in terms of infrastructure, society, or culture, it didn't take me long to realise that both the countries were polar opposites of each other. Back in the day, India was still modernising and the challenges of adjusting in a developing country is another story for another day.

But, it wasn't all that bad. The silver lining was meeting my relatives and basking in the love and hospitality of the Indian culture. It was the first time in my life I felt like I actually belonged somewhere.

Once I returned to the UK, I was welcomed by another surprise. Because of my parent's lack of knowledge and understanding they were not able to make a correct decision for my future. All they said was since I'm already about to complete secondary school, there's no point in continuing further because further education wasn't an option for me.

Even though such a decision might have hurt someone inclinded to study, my circumstances were different. My battle with dyslexia had always been a hurdle in my academic journey, so a part of me was relieved that my suffering was finally over. Was it, though?

Chapter 4
Toxic Marriage

"The Lord is near to those who have a broken heart, and saves such as have a contrite spirit."

Psalms 34:18 NKJV

Goldfishes are beautiful, aren't they? They are such exquisite creatures, but it's quite a pity they can't thrive in the vast sea. Instead, their entire existence revolves around the gentle ripples and reflections of freshwater. Have you ever wondered if these golden swimmers ponder what life might be like in the expansive sea? The truth is, they don't. For goldfish, a pond is their world, which wraps them in a comforting sense of security. The vastness of the world beyond the pond is never a thought that crosses their minds.

My life was much like these goldfish's when I was young. I lived in a big house that I knew very well. My daily routine was consistent, and I didn't know much about the world outside my place. My house was my haven. It was my happy place, making me feel safe and content. I didn't care about the world outside my environment. The analogy beautifully captures the simplicity of my early life, where the idea of venturing beyond the familiar was as unimaginable as a goldfish contemplating life in the vast, open sea.

Something changed as I grew up and got married, left my pond, and ventured into the sea. There, I encountered new experiences, overcame challenges, and learned valuable lessons. I was no longer a goldfish confined to a small world but rather a fish exploring the vast sea. As a result, I began to care about the world beyond my pond.

When the news of my impending marriage reached me at the tender age of 15, it didn't send shockwaves through my world as one might expect. In fact, I welcomed it with open arms. Why? Well, marriage had always been painted as my ultimate destiny, a path I was destined to tread. The promise of a husband, a new home, gifts, and attention set my heart racing with a thrill I couldn't deny.

In today's world, revealing such news to a 15-year-old might be considered a recipe for chaos. But for me, it wasn't upheaval; it was anticipation. You might wonder why, and truth be told, even I couldn't offer a clear answer back then. Honestly speaking, I never thought I had a say in this. It was like a script handed over to me. I did not write it. It was written by generations before me. The fate of every woman in my family was sealed like this decades before we were even born.

Education, career, leisure, and passion were things we never thought about. And why would we? They were not charted courses for us women. We knew our ultimate destiny ever since the beginning. We were supposed to become a good wife, a good mother, and a good daughter-in-law. It was impossible to argue against this traditional route – completely out of question! Instead, our mothers used to train us to embody these roles. Everyone believed that this training would ultimately transform us into better humans too.

A part of me agrees with it, though. I like to believe all that training I received as a kid might have a little something to do with the kind of human I am today. Not to gloat about myself, but I do think of myself as a nice person. Someone who's empathetic. However, back then I did not know that this apparently simple path would dump me into a toxic marriage. I had no idea it will make me question everything that I was taught about my destiny.

But we are not going to talk about the toxicity surrounding my marriage just now. First, I want to clarify that it wasn't all that bad. There were moments, in the beginning, that seemed straight out of a fairy tale, where every day felt like living in a dream, and I basked in the feeling of being on top of the world. Let me take you back to those days when the sun seemed to shine brighter, and every step I took felt like dancing in the air. The early chapters of my marital journey were painted with hues of joy and moments that made my heart flutter with happiness.

Let me rewind the tape to the very beginning, to May 1979, when I got married at the age of sixteen, starting with my grand exit from the familiar comfort of my family home, stepping into the uncharted territory of my new dwelling. To put it plainly, it paralleled the tales I had either envisioned or overheard from the hushed conversations among my married cousins.

Upon setting foot in my husband's home, I was met with an additional array of rituals, accompanied by games and traditional activities that added a layer of intrigue to the whole affair. Amidst these ceremonial undertakings, the anticipation of meeting my husband for the first time created a flutter in my stomach.

In those days, it was customary for the bride to be taken back to her parent's house after all the rituals and ceremonies had taken place. It was only after two weeks, when my husband and his parents came to fetch me that I returned to my marital home and had a union with my husband. When I came back, the wedding celebrations had calmed down, and it was time for me to build relationships and get to know my husband and his family.

I grabbed a bite with my mother-in-law after freshening up. Afterwards, my in-laws took me to my husband's room and I was asked to wait for him to arrive. I was also instructed to not take off my veil. And so, I sat there – all alone – with thousands of questions in my mind. Who was he? What did he look like? What kind of a person is he? Until this point, I wasn't really familiar with what marriage actually meant. If I'm being honest, that was the last thing on my mind. I was too excited with the thought of being alone with a man for the first time in my life.

I had no idea what to expect or do, so I waited patiently. Seconds turned into minutes and minutes into hours, but there was no sign of him. I kept glancing at the wall clock every now and then, wondering what was taking him so long. When he did not arrive even after hours, my nerves got the best of me. Yet, there was nothing I could do.

Then he entered with shyness, not knowing what to do. He put his record player on with songs from the '70s, which actually helped put my emotions at ease. These are precious memories, although we were very young and had no concept of marriage. There was a sense of belonging to each other. He lifted my veil as per custom, and over the next few days, we started to get acquainted with each other, sharing our thoughts, feelings, likes, and dislikes. I learned about his hobby; he enjoyed observing and drawing birds. As the first rays of the morning sun filtered through the window and the melodious chirping of birds filled the air, I woke up from my sweet, peaceful sleep, thinking that all my dreams had come true. There was so much joy within my heart.

I woke up and was lost in my thoughts when I heard a gentle knock on my door, indicating that my mother-in-law was trying to wake me up. I got out of bed, acknowledged her, and got washed and dressed in one of my new outfits before joining her for breakfast. She came across as very pleasant and caring, wanting me to blend in with the family. However, little did I know that she was fighting her own demons, being controlled and abused by my father-in-law. We got to talking, and instructions were poured down on me like raindrops. She

29

gave me guidelines on everything - from how to behave around my husband and father-in-law to kitchen duties.

The initial first few weeks were like a dream come true. Living in Portsmouth near the seaside had its advantages. I would help my mother-in-law prepare a picnic basket for the whole family, and we would all head off to the beach. It was exciting for me to wear a veil from my father-in-law, as it was a sign of respect for the head of the household, according to the Sikh culture. Although this custom was not widely practiced anymore, this family still held it dear. As we strolled along the sunny beach and arcades of the fairgrounds, my in-laws would walk in front of us, and my husband's siblings and I would walk behind them.

I was someone fresh and new on the scene, and everyone wanted to be around me, particularly my husband's siblings. All of them were boys except for my disabled sister-in-law, who was around seven years old at the time. I had the job of caring for her needs on top of my other responsibilities. The boys enjoyed doing boisterous things with me, like wetting me with a hosepipe when I went into the garden. They also wanted me to participate in games like tennis and football in the large garden at the back of the house. Sometimes, they would bring me cream cakes, which made me feel loved and appreciated. However, when things didn't go their way, they would call me all sorts of names under the sun.

We got married in May, and in December 1979, I spent my first Christmas with my spouse's family, away from my own. It was interesting to see the contrasting ways in which each family celebrated Christmas. As it was my first Christmas in my new home, I was pleasantly surprised to receive many gifts from various family members and relatives.

The days following my marriage were not without their challenges. I found myself enjoying a similar status of significance in my husband's home. Now, whether 'privileges' is the right term for it is debatable, but what I'm trying to convey here is that, like me, my husband held the role of the eldest in his family.

Transitioning from one home to another didn't alter my responsibilities – I remained the big 'sister' and 'daughter,' not only to my own siblings but also to my husband's. The shift from tending to my siblings to looking after my husband's brothers and sister felt like a natural progression. Far from being burdensome, I embraced the role wholeheartedly. This caring, supporting, and maintaining the duties of the household was just part of a daughter-in-law's job.

However, one thing I realised during those initial days was that my family and my husband's family were day and night apart. Everything they did here was completely different from the way it was done at my home. Although my mother-in-law was very challenging at times, we did have some fun times doing things together like sewing, gardening, playing tennis and cooking. However, as the initial excitement of the 'honeymoon phase' began to fade, I couldn't help but notice the darker aspects of my new family.

Starting with my husband, he was seldom at home, especially during the night. This bothered me deeply as, after a day filled with chores that took a toll on me both physically and mentally, I longed for familial company. However, I had to sleep alone every night since he was never home at night. He would come back at dawn, reeking of alcohol. At times, he wasn't even aware of his surroundings. Sometimes, he used to just collapse on the bed without taking off his shoes, and I had to put him to bed properly.

When it started, I confronted him. However, I realised the hard way that I shouldn't create a scene. I clearly remember how he yelled at me the first time I called him out. He became incredibly aggressive, yelling at me in a manner I had never experienced before. Faced with the threat of physical violence, I stepped aside, allowing him to do as he pleased. From that day forward, I avoided any attempts at conversation when he was intoxicated, understanding the potential consequences of stirring the waters during those moments.

Yet, in the midst of these perplexing circumstances, I found myself starting to fear what the future really held for me. My in-laws had an old-school mind-set that was even more restrictive than my parents'. They had a very superstitious way of thinking, which was completely off the radar of my thinking.

Time kept passing, and my in-laws grew more comfortable in my presence. Soon, their hushed arguments escalated into full-blown confrontations. Their disagreements reached a point where the once-muted disagreements transformed into loud, heated exchanges, with objects being thrown and the entire house becoming a stage for their uproar disputes.

While they fought on many instances, I particularly remember one incident. It unfolded on an ordinary day, with my husband slumbering away after a night out with his friends. I was in the kitchen, busily preparing lunch, when the doorbell interrupted the routine. Scanning the room for assistance, my mother-in-law discovered that everyone was preoccupied in one way or another. Eager to lend a hand, I suggested leaving the pot on the stove to answer the door, but she declined, opting to address the visitor herself.

Upon opening the door, a stranger stood before her, making inquiries that left her perplexed. Sensing the need for consultation, my mother-in-law summoned my father-in-law. Up to this point, everything seemed ordinary, doesn't it? However, something about the situation triggered my father-in-law in a way that remains unfathomable to me. Suddenly, he became agitated, launching into a harsh outburst as he accused his wife of infidelity and flirting with the mysterious man. The siblings of my husband huddled in a corner, their eyes wide with terror as they witnessed their mother being subjected to a merciless assault. The chaos grew so deafening that even my husband stirred from his slumber, intervened to try and bring about a resolution to the escalating conflict.

On this particular day, a realisation dawned on me that my husband was part of a family that was far from functional. It felt like the missing piece of the puzzle had finally been found, and I could comprehend his nature and personality more deeply. The reason behind his frequent frustration and aloofness started to become clear to me. I began to speculate that perhaps the partying and drinking served as a way to escape from the domestic problems that plagued his household.

I started fearing these loose people in this household. It felt like I was fighting for a lost cause, and I had no idea how to make it matter. I was physically doing everything they wanted me to do, but it clearly wasn't enough. One minute, everything would be calm and peaceful. The next minute, a hurl of physical and verbal abuse would come at me from out of nowhere. There was no discipline in this family. The only person holding the torch was my mother-in-law, leading the males of this household trying to keep order. But she also had a spiteful spirit, wanting me to experience what she and her mother-in-law had gone through. So, she would teach my husband to carry on the tradition of keeping a watchful eye over his wife, which had been passed down for generations. She even told him lies about me by manipulating the truth of my behaviour whilst he was out, misleading him so he would get violent towards me and would physically and verbally abuse me. She didn't hide what she said to him from me, so I knew that her true colours were eventually coming out.

33

The constant, persistent physical abuse that I experienced made me immune to it, and I no longer felt pain when I got hit. Looking back now, I realise that my husband's actions came from his mother's influence on him. When I think of all the nice words he spoke to me initially when we first met, and over the first couple of months as we were getting to know each other, like comparing me to one of his favourite actresses, it didn't match up to the person he had become. He had become a totally opposite person – a stranger I couldn't relate to.

Now that I think of it, it seems like seeing all her daughter-in-laws being controlled and abused pleased my mother-in-law. However, I was the only one at the time and the only one who broke free and conquered my fears, as I will reveal in the following chapters.

The revelation of my mother-in-law's vindictive desire for me was devastating for me. This marked the beginning of a dark chapter. From physical assaults to hurling insults, my husband spared no effort to ensure each day in that house resembled a living nightmare for me, creating scenes for my in-laws to enjoy watching on top of their drama of disputes. Oh, how I missed my family members, even my mother, and the security of my own home I once knew.

Enduring the torment in silence became my daily ordeal, driven by the fear that voicing my pleas would fall on deaf ears, dismissed without a second thought. The dread of being branded as someone with a failed marriage haunted me. Did I desire to wear such a label? Absolutely not. The prospect of tarnishing my parents' reputation and subjecting them to the scrutiny of others, who would question why their daughter faced divorce, was a burden I couldn't bear. And so, I bore the brunt of the harsh treatment from those around me.

I vividly recall a day when the weight of it all became too much to bear. The relentless onslaught pushed me to the brink, prompting a desperate act. Sneaking into my mother-in-law's room, I seized a handful of sleeping pills, swallowing them one by one in a quiet appeal for release from my traumatic existence. Miraculously, I was discovered by my husband and rushed to the hospital in the nick of time. The doctor attributed my survival to sheer luck, and yet, the nightmare of my life persisted.

Communication with my parents was restricted, and honestly, I also embraced that idea partly. I wanted to keep my suffering concealed, and talking to them would risk the exposure of my agonising reality. Yet, in a twist of fate, my parents reached out for me. They urgently summoned me home, citing my mother's ailing health. Stressed and anxious, I implored my husband to take me to them immediately. However, upon arrival, we discovered that my mother was perfectly well. The confusion lifted when she revealed that her ill health was a plan, a ploy to bring me back home after hearing so many negative stories about my well-being.

My husband was honoured and welcomed, being at my side with care and respect within my own family while I endured torment in my marital home. This left me contending with the blatant contrasts of my fractured life. On the surface, all appeared normal. I carefully maintained a facade, laughing and smiling around my parents, ensuring no trace of suspicion crossed their minds. But being away from his family, my husband's behaviour was different almost as if he wanted to be with me and my family genuinely.

In my perception, we presented a flawless illusion of a loving couple. Yet, as the saying goes, you can't deceive the watchful eye of a parent. As time ticked on, my father invited me to his room one day. This came about when my husband was out with my brothers, and my father mentioned needing assistance with a letter to be read and explained to him.

Upon entering his room, I was ushered to sit across from him. At that moment, uncertainty gripped me, unsure of where this unexpected conversation would lead. Nervousness coursed through me, and rightly so. My father and I had never shared those heartfelt daddy-daughter moments before; this was a first-time occurrence. Besides, I was already burdened with concealing so much, lacking the mental space to stage yet another performance. The air in the room was heavy with unspoken tension as the unexpected conversation began to unfold.

Eventually, after a long silence, my father finally urged me to tell him the truth, to share the weight of what had been transpiring in my life. He spoke of the sparkle in my eyes fading, replaced by a haunting gloominess that he sensed... Concerned for his daughter's well-being, he needed to know if my husband and in-laws treated me with the care and respect that I deserved. Looking for an escape, I attempted to divert the conversation, a skill I learned over the months of masking my struggles. Yet, my father was resolute; my attempts at changing the subject were futile. How long could I keep up the charade when my father, almost pleading, begged me to confide in him?

In mere minutes, tears streamed down my cheeks as I spilled the truth about the ordeal Daddy's little girl had been enduring. My father listened with patience, and when my tale reached its conclusion, he wrapped me in a comforting embrace, a gesture that felt like a lifeline. At that moment, I sensed a fraction of the burden on my shoulders lifting. I was not alone; my father stood as my shield.

Family functions were a large part of the Punjabi culture and so my parents found out about my challenges whilst attending them. Before long, armed with the knowledge of my suffering, he confronted my husband, prompting yet another revelation. I was staggered to learn that my husband never desired to marry me; he was coerced and physically compelled by his parents to make me his wife.

36

Amidst this tumult, one burning question dominated my thoughts: If my in-laws were so determined to make me their daughter-in-law, why did they allow me to suffer in silence? Before reaching a resolution, my father granted my husband the opportunity to present his side of the story. With both perspectives laid bare, my father, in a decision that caught me off guard, reached a verdict. A verdict I had not anticipated. He directed my husband to return without me, declaring that I would be staying with my parents from that day onward.

My breath caught in my throat at his decree. Was he truly instructing my husband to initiate a divorce? In our society, divorced women were not commonplace, particularly within our family circles. I couldn't help but contemplate how my father would navigate the prying questions and judgemental glares of society. Yet, my father, a wise man, demonstrated his strategic judgement. He advised my husband to take his time, and when he was genuinely ready to fulfil the role of a husband, he could return to claim me.

Many years have passed since that momentous decision, and even now, as I reflect on the time when my father took a stand on my behalf, my heart swells with pride and gratitude. At the time, it felt like a bird had been set free from its cage. Never could I have imagined that someone would become my shield in such a profound manner. I had resigned myself to a life of despair in that toxic household and marriage.

Little did I know, my fate held far different plans for me. In that fleeting moment, I had no idea where my life would take me. It seemed as though life had hit an abrupt pause, leaving me suspended in the unknown. But it is true that what we comprehend is but a mere drop, while what we don't know is like an endless ocean before us.

Chapter 5
Escaping The Toxicity

"And you shall know the truth, and the truth shall make you free."

John 8:32 NKJV

Have you ever thought about what would happen to an animal that has been in captivity for its entire life, if it were suddenly released into the wild? The answer might surprise you. Circus lions, for instance, have been born and raised in captivity, and as a result, their natural instincts have been suppressed over time. This makes them unable to fend for themselves or hunt for prey if they were to be released into the wild. In other words, they have been domesticated.

This concept is something that I can relate to very well. You see, when my father ordered my husband to return home without me, I felt like I had been thrown into the wild without any idea of how to survive on my own. I was confused, disoriented, and struggling to adapt to my new life without the support of my partner.

However, unlike the circus lion, I managed to survive. It was a challenging journey, and there were days when I felt like I was drowning. But with perseverance, I gradually began to resurface and find my way in this new world.

In the days and weeks that followed my separation from my husband, I experienced a range of emotions - from anger and frustration to sadness and despair. But through it all, I held onto the hope that one day, things would get better. And they did - gradually, but surely, as you will discover in this chapter.

Let's start from the beginning, though. Let me take you back to the moment when my father decided I was not going to return to my marital home. Was I relieved? Scared? Distressed? To this day, I cannot explain what I felt that day. All I know is that it was not easy, especially bidding farewell to my husband.

I watched as he packed up his belongings, stealing glances at me every now and then. I had a feeling deep down that this was the end of our relationship. We were unsure if we would ever see each other again, and even if we did, we had no idea how things would transpire between us.

The moment when he left was one of the most difficult moments of my life. The feeling of watching someone you love leave, as if a part of you is being ripped away, is indescribable. It was as if my world was crumbling down. I waited for him to turn around and look at me one last time, but I was fooled by my hopes yet again. I stood there, letting the feeling of uncertainty overwhelm me, and I struggled to make sense of it all.

Despite the fact that he had treated me quite poorly and barely showed any affection towards me, I still felt a deep sense of belonging towards him. And, somewhere deep down, I think he felt the same way, too. It was a complicated relationship that was difficult to define, but it was also a relationship that had a profound impact on my life.

As I reflect on that moment now, I realise that it was a turning point in my life. It was the moment when everything changed, and I was forced to confront my fears and find a way to move forward. It was a time of great pain and confusion, but it was also a time of immense growth and self-discovery.

After my husband left, I returned to the comfort and safety of my childhood home, surrounded by family who genuinely loved and cared for me. This was a stark contrast to my previous life with my husband, where I often felt like an unpaid servant and was constantly accused of wrongdoing. It was a relief to be able to move around the house without the constant fear of being criticised for something as trivial as the state of a room.

Despite having spent most of my life in this house, returning felt strange, but in a good way. I had forgotten how it felt to be in a place where I was taken care of, and my needs were prioritised. The relief was profound, and I began to feel like I was finally able to breathe again.

My father's home became a haven for me, a place where I could heal from the scars of my previous life. The memories of my marital life still lingered in the form of a few physical scars, but even those began to fade as time passed. I was grateful to be back in a place where I felt safe, loved, and valued.

When I used to reflect on the tumultuous chapter of my life marked by the pain inflicted by my husband and his family, I would have this deep desire to recover, to heal, and to move forward. The wounds were so raw, so profound, that at times, I believed that speaking about them would only reopen them, preventing any chance of closure. I longed to erase that chapter entirely, to be free of its burden, and to reclaim the lightness I once felt.

In my pursuit of healing, I decided to withdraw from conversations about my marriage. I stopped replaying the events in my mind, hoping that I could somehow diminish their power over me by ignoring them. I yearned to feel as liberated internally as I did externally, to shed the weight of sorrow that clung to me.

However, some family members, with all their good intentions, had a different perspective. They believed that healing could only come from openness and sharing. I remember the stream of relatives who came to offer their condolences and support and their persistent encouragement for me to speak up. They wanted me to vocalise my experiences, to shed light on the pain I had endured at the hands of my husband and in-laws.

But did I want to expose and shame them in front of others? No. It was not within my nature to seek retribution or to inflict shame, even upon those who had caused me such deep hurt. Yet, it seemed as though I had little control over my own narrative. I felt like a puppet, with them holding the strings, guiding me towards a path of disclosure that I was not ready to tread.

Despite my reservations, I found myself recounting my story, sharing the pain and the betrayal with those who came to offer their support. Each retelling felt like a reopening of old wounds, a reliving of past traumas.

I had assumed that my struggles were over, but they were far from it. Following the news of my separation, our friends and family flooded us with intrusive questions. Their unforgiving inquiries made my family and me feel uncomfortable and scrutinised. They looked at me with suspicion, as if I were to blame, and casually ridiculed my family for having a daughter with a broken marriage.

I had anticipated that our society could be cruel, but what truly caught me off guard was some my family's response to the taunts and insults that came my way. In the face of such misfortune, I had hoped that they would stand by my side, offer their protection, and be my safe haven. I needed their love and support more than ever before.

Unfortunately, my expectations were shattered when some of them did the exact opposite. Instead of providing me with the comfort and assurance that I so desperately needed, they added to my pain. To make matters worse, they went ahead and spread rumours about me, telling people that I had brought shame to our family and let everyone down. Their words only served to magnify my pain and disappointment, and I was left to deal with the fallout of their actions.

My question is, how was it my fault? How was it my fault that my in-laws treated me poorly? How was it my fault that my husband did not love me? Despite their behaviour, I tried my best to be a good wife to my husband and keep the peace. I cooked for them, cleaned their house, and even did their laundry, but nothing ever seemed to be enough. I had done everything I could to make our marriage work, but it seemed like the more I did, the less it was. And yet, somehow, I was still the one blamed for the failure of our relationship.

As time passed, I began to question myself and wondered if I could have done more to make the situation better. Perhaps if I had put in more effort, things would have been different. The weight of this burden became too much to bear, leaving me feeling small and ashamed of myself. To say the least, I was unhappy with how things turned out.

However, I felt grateful when I compared my current situation to my life at my marital home. I remembered the constant emotional and physical abuse that I had to endure, and the thought of it made my current situation seem like a blessing in disguise. But even with this realisation, I couldn't help feeling like I could have done more to prevent the situation from getting worse.

My mind kept drifting back to those dark days of my life, and negative comments from people took a toll on me, no matter how hard I tried to ignore them. I was at home all day, and there was nothing else to occupy my mind. I felt like I was going crazy, and I knew I needed a distraction. So, I attempted to work so that I could have something else to focus on. However, my family was conservative, and they didn't allow me to work. They believed that it was not a woman's place to work outside the home. I was frustrated, but I understood that I had to respect their wishes.

So, I was stuck in a loop where I now had to take on the role of the eldest daughter in the household, and all my previous responsibilities of doing household chores and taking care of my siblings were back on me. I felt like I was back to square one, and it was demoralising. But I knew that I had to keep going, hoping and waiting for things to improve.

Soon, my father proposed a solution. He presented an idea that was thrilling and terrifying at the same time. He suggested that I should take driving lessons. The thing is, back in my time, it was not common to see women driving. It was a rare occurrence, and my family, being conservative, was hesitant to embrace the idea. However, my father felt restricted without a car and wanted someone in the family to know how to drive.

Enrolling in a driving school was not a decision I took lightly. I always thought that my battles with dyslexia were over ever since I dropped out of school. Little did I know my disability would come back to haunt me when I would take driving lessons. I was not particularly confident in my ability to pass the written tests. As expected, I failed them multiple times. But I refused to give up. I wanted to make my father proud and show him that I could be independent if given the chance.

After several attempts, I finally passed my driving test and obtained my license. It was a momentous occasion for me and my family. I was overjoyed, and my father was especially proud. However, the road to obtaining my license was not easy. I vividly remember the days and nights I spent practising behind the wheel, getting accustomed to the gears and pedals. It was a steep learning curve, but I persevered.

Learning how to drive was a significant milestone for me, and it was more than just making my father proud. It was a moment where

I finally felt like I was worth something and that I could accomplish anything. The road to this achievement was full of obstacles, but I succeeded.

However, learning to drive was just the beginning of a series of positive changes in my life. It was like a big transformation that changed the dynamics within our family. My father and I explored countless used car dealerships in the town, and after a lot of searching, we finally found the perfect car for our use. Although shopping for a car was harder than we initially thought, it was a fun and exciting experience.

As I started spending more time behind the wheel, I grew more confident. I was now responsible for dropping off my siblings, taking my mother shopping, and driving my father to different places. These tasks were once mundane chores, but now they were exciting opportunities that kept me busy and helped me grow as a person.

Despite all this, there was something amiss. It felt like my heart was hollow, and a piece of the puzzle was yet to be found. At first, I tried to ignore it, but the feeling kept growing so much that even my family took notice of it. So, we decided to try something different – explore our spirituality.

A new chapter began in my family's journey when they started exploring faiths beyond our own Sikh beliefs, guided by a sense that a higher power was intervening in their lives. We set out on a quest, attending various religious movements where people sought solace and guidance in their moments of desperation. Each of these faiths had its own set of practices, each offering a path to seek help but often requiring some form of payment in return.

Reflecting on these experiences, I realised that my parents, like many others, were searching for meaning and solutions in a world filled with uncertainties. They were dealing with cultural beliefs and struggling to discern right from wrong in the complexity of human society. These experiences painted a picture in my mind—a picture of life's struggles and the belief that to navigate them, one must seek help from sources beyond the tangible world.

The decision to renovate our large family home came after some experiences that had inspired us. We decided to segregate the two attics and convert one of them into a private space for prayers and reflection. The room was designed to accommodate people of all faiths, and we adorned it with pictures and statues representing various faiths. We even added a cross symbolising Jesus to respect the Christian faith.

My father was a devout Sikh, and he remained steadfast in his beliefs despite the diversification in our household. Therefore, he decided to separate all the Sikh devotional items and placed them in another corner of the room. This was his personal space where he would spend time praying. He would meditate, recite his prayers, and immerse himself in his faith.

From a very young age, my siblings and I were taught by our parents about the importance of acknowledging a higher power in our lives. Every morning, we would gather as a family and begin our day with a sense of gratitude and a deep awareness of God's presence. Our parents believed that this daily practice would help us cultivate a sense of gratefulness, humility, and spiritual connection that would stay with us throughout our lives.

As part of our family's cultural and religious traditions, we would visit the Sikh temple every Sunday. The temple was a place of great beauty and serenity, with its shimmering gold domes and intricate carvings. Inside, we would be greeted by the soothing sounds of the harmonium and tabla and the mesmerising voices of the kirtan singers.

The focal point of the temple was the Guru Granth Sahib, the holy book of the Sikh faith. The book was kept on a raised platform, covered in rich fabrics and adorned with flowers. We would sit cross-legged on the floor, with our heads covered as a sign of respect, and listen to the recitation of the hymns from the Guru Granth Sahib. The hymns were sung in a melodic and rhythmic style, with each line repeating the same melody to create a sense of unity and harmony.

As I faced various challenges while growing up, I began to question the very purpose of our existence. I constantly pondered about the nature of life and why we have to face difficulties. These thoughts consumed me to the point where I felt lost and didn't know where to turn for guidance.

It was during this time of uncertainty that I found solace in visiting a church whenever I was alone. I felt a sense of calm, as if the walls of the church held the secrets to life's mysteries. I would spend hours in prayer, seeking answers to the questions that plagued me.

One day, I entered a church without knowing its denomination. I spoke to a priest about my struggles in my marriage and sought guidance. To my surprise, he advised me to go to a marriage counselling agency. This was a turning point in my life as the support and guidance I received there helped me to understand my situation better and find a way forward.

Through this experience, I began to explore my faith and discovered a newfound sense of purpose. It made me wonder, was this my true calling?

Chapter 6
The Roots Of Abuse

"For I will restore health to you And heal you of your wounds,' says the Lord, 'Because they called you an outcast saying: "This is Zion; No one seeks her."

Jeremiah 30:17 NKJV

Abuse. It is a small word, isn't it? But don't let the simplicity of the terminology fool you. Abuse can be like a contagious virus that continues to spread from person to person, causing no good. Or perhaps, you can think of it as the weed that grows in a garden behind your back and chokes out the healthy plants, leaving nothing but destruction in its wake. Like poison, it drips into every aspect of a man's life, damaging and corrupting everything it comes in contact with.

But what does abuse really mean? It's a topic that sparks debate and differing opinions. Some associate it with substances like drugs, while others connect it with objects or institutions. Yet, through my experiences, I've learned that abuse is not limited to specific things. It's the mistreatment or misuse of almost anything—whether it's relevant or not.

As I pen down this chapter, reflecting on my life, I can't help but wonder why people resort to abuse. After much thought, I could only reach one verdict. I've concluded that selfishness lies at the heart of it. While there may be various reasons behind abusive behaviour, selfishness often plays a significant role. It's that burning desire to hurt others when things don't go as planned, a desire that stems from self-centeredness.

I believe that most of the time, we act out of fear – the fear of judgement. What will people think? This desire to seek approval from others is the sole motivation behind many of our actions. But what if I told you that there was a better way to live? One that frees you from this fear and allows you to be yourself truly.

Another conclusion that I have drawn from my experiences is that abusive traits are inherited. They are not just suddenly bestowed upon anyone. Instead, they are passed from one generation to the next within families. It's like a never-ending cycle, a vicious circle that seems difficult to break.

And the only way to break this cycle is by enlightening yourself. Becoming self-aware. I often think of it as a light bulb illuminating a dark room or a candle flame dispelling shadows —the analogy, in my opinion, perfectly captures the importance of acquiring the right knowledge and understanding. How could one lead a productive, fulfilling, and meaningful life without them?

Now, I started having these thoughts quite a while ago – when I returned to my parents and started exploring different faiths – to be precise. By this time, I had endured all forms of abuse, be it mental, physical, emotional, or verbal. But I was still far from doing anything about it. And what could I do? I was just starting to test my strength.

It had been three long years since I last laid eyes on my husband, my life partner. During this time, I stayed at my parents' home with absolutely no communication with him. The fate of our marriage hung in the balance and the future looming over us was uncertain. It was only in 1982 that our families got back in touch and started thinking about our future. Finally, after much deliberation, it was decided that my husband and I should give our marriage another shot. Now this decision wasn't taken because it was better for both of us. Rather, it was considered the only way to restore the honour and prestige of both the families. Divorce was out of the question as for my family, it would signify that I have no character. My husband's family, on the other hand, saw it as an opportunity for restoring their own reputation since it had been ruined in our society due to the news of how I was mistreated.

But this decision to reunite wasn't made just like that. It took a lot of time, thought and consideration. It required us to accept our differences and try to find a middle ground to make our marriage work. We were supposed to overcome the obstacles that caused us to drift apart in the first place. So, it goes without saying, this certainly wasn't an easy task. However, both of us were willing to give it our best shot.

Once all things were settled, my husband came to pick me up from my parents' house along with his family. I packed my bags and left with them towards Doncaster, our new home, since my in-laws had moved out of Portsmouth. A part of me wondered if the change of location had also brought a change to the environment in their household, but I was disappointed to learn that things were quite similar as to how I left them. The good thing, however, was that the arguments between my mother-in-law and father-in-law had toned down a bit.

That's not even the best part, though. I was also quite pleased to notice a huge change in my husband's behaviour and attitude towards me. He wasn't the same distant and aloof man anymore. Instead, I could feel that he was trying to put more effort into our marriage in order to make it work. Surprisingly, he even started initiating open conversations with me – something that I had always longed for. I was glad to see that he, too, wanted to make things work between us.

We started talking and the more we talked, the more I realised that my husband and I are no longer the naïve, young 16-year-olds we were at the time of our marriage. It almost felt like this time apart had help us grow and mature in various ways. Our way of thinking had significantly evolved since we last shared the same roof.

I also learned that he had been living alone in Doncaster for the past three years. We began catching up on everything we missed out on and he shared the struggles he encountered after moving out of his parents' home. According to him, the constant bickering and violence had become too much for him to bear, which is why he moved away in the first place. However, he had only returned after I decided to come back.

For the first time in my marital life, it actually felt like I was getting to know the man I was wedded off to. It was wonderful to hear him talk about what went on in his life after we fell apart. Even though he had faced considerable challenges, I believe it was all worth it. His experiences had grown him in many ways and he was now a stronger person; someone who was ready to be a husband.

With time, we started to get along better and apparently, it looked like our marriage would end up working out. We were spending more and more time together, enjoying each other's company and the little things in life. We even started going out alone for shopping and dinners. It might seem ordinary to some people but for us, it was a luxury we were not allowed before. After a long time, I was once again hopeful about my future we were finally on the right track.

However, one day after everyone had fallen asleep, my husband and I were casually talking in our bedroom, casually laughing and joking around. Suddenly, someone knocked loudly on the door. Before we could answer, my mother-in-law came in, looking very angry. I don't know what made her so upset even to this day. She started accusing us of things without any proof. She even said I was drunk, even though I wasn't.

She was so angry that she told us to leave her house because there was no space for us. It was very sad and surprising, and we didn't know why she was treating us like that. My husband and I were very confused, hurt, and felt like we were betrayed by his mother's sudden outburst. We didn't know what to do.

We couldn't understand what was happening and we didn't think there was even a slight chance that things would get better. We were so done living in this toxic environment. So, we decided to leave the house right away. But, when we tried to go out, we found out that my mother-in-law had locked all the doors. We couldn't leave our own home.

How could it be? It was hard for me to believe that someone could do that to us. My husband, however, didn't want to give up and suggested we escape through the kitchen window. I was scared but knew it was our only chance to leave before things got worse.

We didn't have much time, so we packed only the most important things for our trip. Then my husband left to buy tickets to Wolverhampton, where my parents lived. I was overcome with fear, but I knew it was the right decision for our safety. While he was gone, I felt really nervous and worried. I kept checking out the window, hoping to see him coming back, but the street was always empty. I couldn't help but imagine the worst possible scenarios. What if something bad had happened to him? It was hard to stay calm and focused without him there.

After what seemed like a really long time, my husband came back with the tickets. We checked them carefully because we didn't want any problems. When we were sure that everything was okay, we got ready to make our big exit. Even though it was exciting, we also had some adventures and unexpected things happen along the way.

We tried to be really quiet as we went down the stairs so we wouldn't wake anyone up. But things didn't go as planned. My husband accidentally bumped into something and it fell on the floor, expectedly making a loud noise. It echoed through the floor, and woke up my father-in-law. We heard him ask, "Who's there?" in an annoyed voice from his room.

Frozen in our spot, we silently prayed he does not come out of the room. Meanwhile, my husband quickly explained it was just him going to the bathroom, and then it was quiet again. Restoring our breaths, we continued as per plan, ready for whatever lay ahead.

We rushed towards the kitchen, all the while my heart was beating with excitement and nervousness. The moment we slipped out of the kitchen window, it felt surreal. Was this truly happening? It was all dark and silent, yet for some reason, it did not feel creepy. In fact, the occasional rustling of leaves and the cool breeze felt refreshing and soothing. Were we finally free? Sometimes I wonder if we had more time, we might have stayed there a bit longer to appreciate the beauty of the moment. However, we had a train to catch before our in-laws learn about our escape.

Finally, we reached the station and hopped onto the train. Once we found our seats and settled in, the reality of what we just did began to sink in. We finally managed to escape. We were free to live lives on our own terms, away from the controlling nature of my in-laws. This was the last thing that I expected when I came back to live with these dysfunctional people. I felt a strange sense of joy overcoming me, and for the first time in a long time, I felt truly alive.

By the time the train pulled into the station in Wolverhampton, I was filled with anticipation. I couldn't wait for this new chapter in my life to begin as I was hopeful it would be a good change for us. It was early in the morning, and my husband and I decided to take a cab to my parent's home.

Now I don't precisely remember who answered the door when we arrived at my parent's home, but I do remember everyone was shocked to see us so early in the morning. Once we told them about the reason for our sudden arrival, they were relieved and happy to have us home safe and sound. My husband shared he no longer wanted to return to his Doncaster and wanted to start a new life here with me.

My parents were understanding and supportive and welcomed us both with open arms. We spent the next few days adjusting in our new surroundings, exploring the city, and getting to know our new neighbours. It was like a fairy tale - everything seemed perfect. Little did I know that our challenges were not yet over. We were about to enter a phase that would test our relationship and commitment to each other.

Just when I thought the dark chapter of my life was officially over, my husband's monstrous behaviour and his drinking started again. This time is was worse than before. He would often stumble in, completely intoxicated, and the next morning he would have no memory of the previous night. Reluctant to involve my parents, I endured, believing that everything else in our life together was perfect. After all, a bit of compromise seemed a small price to pay for our otherwise happy family life. Besides, having witnessed my father-in-law's abusive and controlling behaviour towards my mother-in-law, I felt resigned to my fate, believing my husband had inherited these traits and was beyond change.

Despite the challenges, I tried to draw closer to him, hoping to understand him better and perhaps help him overcome his drinking habit. As our bond grew stronger, I learned shocking truth about my husband: He was also dyslexic, and his learning difficulties were far more severe than my own. It did not help that his parents were in the real estate business, so all the buying and selling of houses had them moving quite often. Hence, he never had the chance for a stable or undisrupted education.

Whenever I start piecing together all the things that went wrong in my marriage, I can't help but think about my mother's role in it. While I don't doubt her intentions, not for a second, she did have a role to play in how things played out with my husband. Considering the turmoil I had faced, she would constantly advise me to keep looking over my shoulder. She discouraged the fact that I wanted to trust my husband. Looking back, I think this created more tension in our home. I didn't want my husband to become aware of my mother's opinions, so I always acted like a referee, balancing their relationship to ensure peace in the home.

I was already carrying a load of emotional and mental burdens and this dynamic, unfortunately, only added fuel to the fire. I tried my best to keep the peace, yet, my husband's occasional violent outbursts made it harder to manage. Constantly staying in hot water with these relationships soon took a toll on me and I began longing for solace and understanding that seemed out of question during that time.

A few months later, I discovered I was pregnant. This joyful news brought back the good times that I have been craving for. Everyone in my life from my husband to my parents were overjoyed. I was over the moon too. I couldn't wait to step into motherhood and start a family with my husband. My father decided it was about time that my husband and I got our own place.

At the time, my husband and I were not financially stable enough to invest in property, but my father offered to help. He gave the deposit for our new home and even became the guarantor for our mortgage payments. Had it not been for him, we would never be able to purchase a home and call it our own so soon.

Meanwhile, my husband was in search for jobs. Although it took some time, he finally landed one and it was a big day for us. We could finally afford our own expenses! It felt like our lives were changing for the better, and we were headed in the right direction.

However, fate wasn't yet kind to us. My mother never stopped controlling me and the arguments between my husband and I did not dial down either. Despite this, I considered our unborn baby a beacon of hope. I spent all my time hoping that the birth of our child would eventually end all of this – the future excited me and I strongly believed it only held good things for me and my growing family.

Throughout my pregnancy, my husband's drinking and making holes in the walls and doors continued. I tried my best to keep this dark side of my marriage hidden from my family, but they would sometimes find out about it. On several occasions, my father and some other family members tried to talk to and counsel my husband to help him change his bad habits, but to no avail.

Eventually, it was decided that taking him to a doctor would be the best thing to help him. And it did help him for a while, and it quietened him. However, those days were short-lived since he would return to his old self the minute he would start drinking again. Now that I think about it, I don't blame him for anything, really. Like me, he, too, was a broken life. Neither of us knew how to live, yet we tried the best we could.

I found it incredibly challenging to maintain the façade of happiness. It felt like I had to put on a mask every morning and pretend that everything was okay, even when it wasn't. My life was a lie as every morning when I woke up, I was supposed to pick the broken pieces of myself and suppress the turmoil brewing within me.

The burden I was carrying was something only I could see – everyone else was living in oblivion.

The pain I was going through was immense and keeping up appearances in front of everyone else became unbearable for me. After all, how could I maintain the perfect image of happiness when my heart was breaking into pieces? Even though I had people around, I was living all alone because nobody else truly understood what I was going through.

Reminding myself every day to put on a brave face and smile even when I felt like crying was getting too exhausting, and it consumed every inch of my being. All I wanted was someone to confide in, someone I could share my pain with, someone who could offer me comfort. Was this too much to ask? It definitely felt like so at the moment because I was going through the worst phase of my life alone.

However, the day I gave birth to my baby was one of the happiest days of my life. My baby boy was perfectly healthy and when I held him in my arms for the first time, I was overwhelmed with joy. My husband, parents, and siblings were also elated. We received a number of gifts, cards, and phone calls from relatives who couldn't wait to meet the newest addition in our family.

As a new mother, the contentment motherhood brought me was significant. I was responsible for looking after my child's physical needs while my husband would take him out for swimming or fishing. We had divided our responsibilities this way and it worked perfectly well for us.

Life continued, and we welcomed two sons and two daughters into the world. Being a mum to four beautiful children, I could never pick a favourite – even if I tried. All of them hold a special place in my heart and I love and cherish them equally. In fact, I believe it was the love I have for them that kept me going even during the darkest days of my life. It did not matter how difficult my circumstances were, I was a strong and hopeful person as long as I was surrounded by my children.

Everything changed throughout all these years. But if anything remained constant, it was my husband's intoxication. I was confused and frustrated. I had given my best to make him quit drinking yet it was to no avail. I never understood why it was so difficult for him to give up this habit. We all cope with life's challenges in different ways, perhaps this was his. Whatever the reason, he eventually turned into an unpleasant person to talk to. His controlling personality was becoming unbearable.

It was like the word compromise did not exist in his dictionary. It was either his way or highway. Every time, he would make decisions without considering anyone's opinion. It didn't matter if his decisions concerned me or his children, he always had the final say in everything.

But that wasn't all. If sometimes things didn't go the way he wanted them to, he would make an annoying grunting noise to disturb us. Back then I did not realise this, but now I believe this was a form of abuse too.

For instance, one time we were going out, and I was wearing a modest outfit. It wasn't revealing or anything, but he wanted me to cover myself with a coat. I didn't want to do it but he didn't care. He only wanted me and the children to obey him. Even though I had become habitual of this behaviour, it was still a challenge to deal with. I was tired of walking on eggshells around him, not knowing what could set him off next. It was emotionally draining and really disturbed my mental health.

With our children growing up, we needed a larger home. Hence, we started looking for one and eventually bought a lovely 3-bedroom home near my parents' home. It was the perfect location considering how near it was to the children's school. My parents took the responsibility of walking to and from school. It was my dad particularly who loved this new routine. Unfortunately, he couldn't continue with it for long.

Just a few months after we moved into our new home, a tragedy struck our family. My father, only 52 at the time, suddenly passed away. His sudden death was a shock to all of us and we were devastated. It took a long time for us to finally accept that he really was gone. Even after all these years, we deeply miss his presence and love. His death left a void in our lives that I don't think anything could ever fill.

By the time my eldest son turned seven and my daughters were three years old and nine months old, my husband's parents contacted us out of the blue. We hadn't been in touch with them for quite a while now and it was surprising to hear from them so suddenly. They wanted to meet their grandchildren, something I was initially hesitant to allow. A part of this was due to my mother as the believed inviting them back to our lives would only mean more pain for me.

Even though I wasn't particularly fond of this idea in the beginning, I later realised it would be unfair to keep my husband away from his parents. We decided to give it a shot by just my husband visiting them alone. As things improved, we gradually started visiting them together as a family.

Meeting them after all these years, it surprised us to see the way their lives have changed. Some of my husband's siblings were now married, and their family had grown. Their family dynamics had shifted as well and we did not experience any undue focus or pressure.

In fact, if I'm being honest, it even felt warm to be back there. They welcomed us back with open arms and showered our children will love and care.

I later realised this reunion was much needed since it brought me closure and healing. It made me believe that people and situations can change for the better with time. As the saying goes, time heals all wounds and I now believe it can also bring people together.

While I accept reuniting with them was a positive experience, I couldn't help but notice that their home still had the same abusive and controlling environment. But I was grateful to no longer be a part of it. It was wonderful to be able to pick and choose whenever I wanted to go and visit them.

The challenges in my marriage were already enough for me, I did not want any added pressure. However, reconciling with my husband's family did bring some peace to our marriage and relationship.

Chapter 7
Finding Solace In Faith

"If you love Me, keep My commandments. And I will pray the Father, and He will give you another Helper, that He may abide with you forever— the Spirit of truth, whom the world cannot receive because it neither sees Him nor knows Him; but you know Him, for He dwells with you and will be in you. I will not leave you orphans; I will come to you."

John 14:15-21NKJV

As the saying goes, when the going gets tough, the tough gets going. In my case, it certainly holds true to some extent. I was at a stage of life where I had finally accepted a perfect marriage would always be a pipe dream for me.

I had finally come to terms with the fact that my life isn't a fairy tale. I wasn't born a Cinderella who was destined to live happily ever after with her Prince Charming. Instead, I was born to compromise – for the sake of society, my parents, and my marriage. And so, compromise I did.

Years passed by, and I stopped wondering if things would ever get better in my marriage. Granted, they were better than how it started, but after a certain point, it felt futile to hope for further betterment. And if I'm being honest, I had kind of adjusted myself to this 'new normal'.

However, I couldn't help but feel a void. It felt like something was missing in my life, and I couldn't figure out what it was. My mother, on the other hand, was persistent in saying that this was because we have yet to discover a higher source of peace, comfort, and solace.

She remained persistent in her search throughout all these years. I would often find her attending different places in search of a beacon of light that would illuminate our dark circumstances – she was desperate for a way out of our situation.

Meanwhile, she did not forsake the Sikh faith, though. I mean, how could she? We lived in a community, and we were bound to follow its patterns. So, even when she continued her search, she did not abandon the thinking patterns of her ancestral mind-set stooped in tradition, culture, and superstitions.

Despite exploring other faiths, my mother never held any disregard for Sikhism – or any other faith, for that matter. She held high reverence for them all. However, it felt like we all were merely living a life of ignorance and following in the footsteps of our community's ancestors, staying perfectly in line with the patterns that have continued for generations.

It took me a long time to realise that faith is not just an interest followed by devotion. It's way more than that. It's man's effort to reach God, to connect with Him. Come to think of it, Christianity doesn't fall in this spectrum. Rather, I believe it is God's message – a message full of love – destined to reach His people.

There were times when my mother would want me to accompany her to the different religious gatherings she would visit. Sometimes, I would tag along, and other times, I would just wait for her outside in the car. Apparently, I was perfectly alright, but deep down, I sensed this sensitivity to the spiritual realm. This led me to experience so many things that I can't describe in words.

At one point, I no longer felt the need to find a God. In fact, I wasn't even sure there existed one. After all, if there was a God, why would He want to put me through all these terrible things, one by one? I started convincing myself that faith is nothing but a lie that we tell ourselves to put a bandage over our wounds. Oh, how ignorant was I?!

God never left me alone, though. Soon after, my paths crossed with a group of believers – the Jehovah Witnesses. Little did I know that those numbered encounters I had with them during my low moments would ultimately end up changing my life for the better.

Out of nowhere, I had a feeling in my heart that the only way God could hear my pleas was through the prayers of a Christian person. I realise how that sounds, but coming from where I came from, it made perfect sense to me at that moment. Hence, I started opening up to them more. One thing led to another, and I soon found myself learning about the Bible from my Christian acquaintances.

Reading the Bible wasn't as simple as I had thought. I found plenty of information from the sacred text, and it got me thinking: Is the way to God truly through the Christian faith? Initially, I couldn't bring myself to accept this truth. It was the first time in my life that something had challenged me so deeply. All the while, I kept wondering if that was true do I even exist at all? All my life, I have been revolving around meaningless rules and rituals, and it took me ten whole years to finally learn who I actually am.

Mind you, this wasn't the first time I had come across Christianity. Along the way, I was handed leaflets or was whispered gentle words about Jesus, but my mind was never capable enough to connect all the dots until I grew acquainted with Jesus personally.

It all started thanks to a friend of mine, who lived right across from me, where we bought our first home. I knew her from secondary school, and she was a born-again Christian. Oftentimes, she would knock on my door and take me to the church. She even took my children to Sunday school, which felt like a much-needed break from parenting at that time. But now that I look back, I realise they were all quite precious moments of blessing them.

Had it not been for my friend and her family, I don't think I would be born again as a Christian and would be walking on the right path. She often remarked, "Rani, I've noticed that every time you're feeling low, you call me to pray for you." She wasn't wrong; I felt a strange sense of belonging to the Christian faith, and I believed my prayers would be answered if she communicated with God on my behalf.

It wasn't long before I started having my own encounters with God. It was during the time I was pregnant with my last born and was studying with the Jehovah Witnesses. I had requested a Bible of my own from the Gideon Bible Society, and I started reading it. Back then, I didn't know ways to connect with Jesus, so I would use the Sikh praying beads and chant and sing Jesus's name and psalms in the Bible.

The deep sense of peace and comfort reading the Bible brought me a feeling that something powerful was happening within me. I started to feel a connection to Jesus that I had never felt before, and I found myself drawn to his teachings.

Although I was exploring my faith, deep down, I knew I had landed on something truly special. The random coincidences I encountered during this period further reaffirmed my belief in this.

For instance, I clearly remember the time we took the kids to the beach, and a random woman bumped into me and handed me a pamphlet about Jesus and the path to salvation. As I replay all these memories, I can't believe how many signs and opportunities Jesus Christ threw my way to bring me to the right path. After all of this, how could I ignore what fate had been telling me? I finally converted to Christianity and accepted Jesus Christ as my Lord and Saviour.

But life wasn't exactly perfect after I declared my new faith. I started experiencing discomfort with some of the requisites this new faith brought with itself. Besides, I had recently given birth, so all the recent developments in my life were too overwhelming to deal with.

At a point, I even considered getting away from Christianity, but I would always be stopped by something or someone who would challenge my troubled heart and mind. It took me a while, but ultimately, I was entirely convinced that Jesus is our true God. In fact, there's even a passage in the Bible about worshipping an unknown God:

"For as I was passing through and considering the objects of your worship, I even found an altar with this inscription: TO THE UNKNOWN GOD. Therefore, the One whom you worship without knowing Him, I proclaim to you: "God, who made the world and everything in it, since He is Lord of heaven and earth, does not dwell in temples made with hands. Nor is He worshipped with men's hands, as though He needed anything since He gives to all life, breath, and all things. And He has made from one blood every nation of men to dwell on all the face of the earth, and has determined their pre-appointed times and the boundaries of their dwellings, so that they should seek the Lord, in the hope that they might grope for Him and find Him, though He is not far from each one of us." **(Acts 17:23-27 NKJV)**

Moving forward, I would experience misunderstanding from my new faith every now and then. It wasn't that I did not believe in the existence of God. I merely wanted to learn more about Him. I wanted to learn what makes Him different?

Perhaps aware of my inner turmoil, He soon intervened and led me through the right path. It was one fine night in January 2006 when I was watching the television, switching channels to find something interesting. Suddenly, something caught my attention. It was a Christian woman giving her testimony on how her faith had helped invite peace into her life. Hearing her describe her experiences in detail, I couldn't stop myself from dialling the number on the screen and conversing with the host.

I got to talking to the lovely lady, and I told her all about my pursuit of God and how I have explored various faiths, hoping to restore my inner peace and solace. Out of frustration and helplessness, I exclaimed, "Why is God not hearing me?"

Her reply was soothing and gentle. She said, "God can hear you loud and clear. It is you who are not hearing God because of all this religious stuff that you have got in the way." Then, she asked if she could pray for me, and I gave her the green signal. As she started praying, I cannot even begin to explain the calmness and peace I felt.

I suddenly felt a fragrance of freshness surrounding me, and I knew something wonderful was about to happen. The lady then proceeded to ask me if I was ready to receive Jesus as my Lord and Saviour.

"Yes, I do." This was all I could manage to utter before I started verbally praying and asking Jesus to come into my heart.

As if the Holy Spirit could hear my pleas, I felt like it was speaking back to me. It was telling me to do something. It asked me to remove the bangle on my wrist that represents another faith. The moment I took it off, I received another prompt to remove what was tied around my arm. Once I had removed all ornaments that displayed my association with my past faith, I suddenly felt this urge to proclaim the prayer, "I am a Sinner saved through the shedding blood of Jesus

Christ who died on the cross for me and that I am surrendering everything to him and I am asking him to be my Lord and Saviour. I believed Jesus was raised from the dead on the third day to restore that was lost."

Now, this may sound ordinary to someone who hasn't witnessed this transformation. But for me, it was a life-altering moment, one that still gives me such encouragement when I think about it. As the Bible says, once you confess, you're born again, and your old self goes away. I can't possibly summarise my experience any better than this.

It was like the darkness that had surrounded me had suddenly vanished, and I was in a completely different realm now where God's spirit had illuminated my surroundings. I could feel the noticeable shift in my perspective, and I knew things were about to get better from this point on.

In Hebrews 11:1, God says, "Faith is the substance of things hoped for, of things not yet seen." I couldn't agree more. My re-birth felt like a road to recovery. It was as if I had turned away from my sinful nature and started doing things the right way, just like how God wanted me to.

But the question is, has my life been constantly uphill since then? No, it certainly was not. However, my faith in Jesus allowed me to stay steadfast in all the battles I have encountered since then, and mind you, I have never been disappointed.

Over time, I also found a way to get to know God better. It was with me all the time. I was just not wise enough. Although it did take me a while, I gradually realised that the Bible is the way to get closer to Jesus. It holds the key to unlocking hidden treasures that brought peace, healing, and deliverance to my life.

Now that I'm recalling my life's events, I particularly remember how challenging it was for me to find my feet in Church as a new believer. Initially, I would go to different churches in search of comfort, but even though every visit brought a sense of peace, the solace I needed was still missing. I believe part of it is because new believers and converts, like me, are unable to find enough support in churches.

What worked for me was taking long walks or spending time in the comfort and security of my own home. I would think of all the questions in my mind over and over again, trying to figure it all out. While there was a lot to be discovered in my newfound faith, I loved how I always felt God and His peace close to me.

The last church I attended served as another turning point in my life. I made a close friend there and did an alpha course with her. Our friendship did not end after the course was completed. We stayed in touch even after that. I would always reach out to her to share my church experiences, and she was kind enough to pray for me and even pay me visits along with her family. This made our bond grow stronger. It was she who invited me to a Bible College where she was already enrolled in a second-year program.

Knowing my struggles with learning, I was hesitant at first, but then I thought, what's the harm in checking it out? The moment I entered the class, my heart was filled with warmth, and I immediately felt a sense of belonging. It felt as if God was telling me He could see how broken I was. I was instantly convinced that I was supposed to be in this place, so I signed up right away.

At first, I only enrolled in the night school, which held classes a few nights a week. However, after six months, I concluded that this wasn't enough and that I needed to spend more time here. But how could I? I was a care support worker back in the day, working 60 hours a week. Yet, I felt so drawn to the place that I ended up giving up my job and enrolled in college full-time for five days a week for three years, and every second was worth it. I hold so much regard for the time I spent in that place, even today, after so many years.

I got to learn countless valuable lessons from people my age as well as those older than me, but two of them actually stuck with me. The first one is the unconditional love of God. As humans, we often mess up, and fellow humans are not often fans of forgiveness. But Jesus doesn't hold anything against us. He loves us despite our flaws and mistakes, and we can always run back to Him.

The other one was learning that Jesus is our righteousness because He paid the price for our sins with His precious blood. I used to believe that being good and doing good was the way to approach God, but after learning this, I realised that it's, in fact, my faith in Jesus that sets me free. I realised nothing can ever come between my relationship with Him – not my family, society, or anything in between.

But that's not all that I learned. I learned about God, myself, people, and relationships. My time at school also taught me the significance of forgiveness. Now, forgiveness, you see, is a tricky concept. You might say you've forgiven someone, but were you able to truly do it with your heart? And to do so, you have to master not getting offended or letting people get the best of you.

Along the way, I also realised that the only way I can make these things happen is by setting boundaries to guide my heart. As believers of Jesus Christ, we're supposed to determine how much access we allow people or even God into our lives, our hearts, our minds, and our emotions. It's all really about how much you're willing to surrender in a relationship, be it with God or people.

Another deeper realisation that I had was perhaps the way I felt God asking me to draw a line, keep all my relationships on one side, and keep Him and me on another. And that's what I did. I started to preserve my relationship with God and keep it separate from all other worldly relationships, even that with my husband and children.

This slight shift in my perspective was a game-changer. It allowed me to look at my personal relationships the way I want them to be. I was no longer a bitter person, getting offended by the remarks of people around me.

Instead, I had entirely applied the truth of the Bible in my life, which taught me how and when to say NO. After all, I'm worth way more than what I have been given in many relationships.

It's one thing to be a compassionate and kind person. However, it's completely another to let people have complete control over you. I learned how to set boundaries, and so should you. Ask yourself, am I opening unnecessary doors?

Chapter 8
Shifting Perspectives

"Oh, taste and see that the Lord is good; Blessed is the man who trusts in Him!"

Psalms 34:8 NKJV

Does it ever feel like your life is nothing but a complicated jigsaw puzzle with pieces scattered all around? That's how I felt for the longest time. I didn't know what my role was in life, and it seemed like everything was happening to me rather than me making things happen. But then, something amazing happened. I found Jesus Christ as my Lord and Saviour, and my life changed forever. It was like finding that one missing puzzle piece that made everything else fall into place.

I know it may sound like I'm taking credit for the change in my life, but the truth is, I can't take any credit at all. It was the Holy Spirit of God that drew me to Himself. Without Him, I would still be lost and wandering aimlessly, searching for peace and solace. I know it may seem crazy to some, but for me, it's the greatest story ever told.

Once I finally accepted the invitation to Jesus, my life did a 180-degree about-turn. Now, it wasn't instant, as you see in movies, but it happened slowly and eventually. My faith in Jesus gifted me with a new perspective on life. It allowed me to view my circumstances with a different lens.

I stopped seeing myself as this poor, helpless woman. Instead, I started believing that I could face anything this life throws at me. I'm not a quitter. I'm a survivor. A survivor who has God on her side. And that there is nothing to worry about when the Creator of Heaven and Earth is by my side. What's going to hold me back?

I knew I had to change my mind-set if I wanted improvement in my actions and outlook towards life. In the Bible, we are encouraged to be hopeful and confident in Jesus about life. That's what the Bible preaches. It opposes self-pity, and knowing that this is what I've been doing all my life, I realised it's time to stop if I want to turn my life around. This became my sole motivation to pursue my goals, not let minor setbacks hold me back, and conquer my fears and anxiety.

I realised that everything in life flows from the intimate relationship I have with Father, Son, and the Holy Spirit. The quiet, intimate moments set us up to face each day. It wasn't like I suddenly stopped worrying about the major and minor problems in my life. I still used to feel stressed out at times. Whenever I used to be in a problem, I would meditate on the Bible, have casual conversations with God, and keep praying to Him. Eventually, all my overthinking would vanish, and I would find this new confidence in God and His message.

I started personalising the messages in the Bible, believing that it was written particularly for my eyes. That those messages were saying something that would happen to me. For instance, the Bible says,

"For I know the thoughts that I think toward you, says the Lord, thoughts of peace and not of evil, to give you a future and a hope. Then you will call upon Me and go and pray to Me, and I will listen to you." **(Jeremiah 29:11-12 NKJV)**

And:

"Everyone who is called by My name, Whom I have created for My glory; I have formed him, yes, I have made him." **(Isaiah 43:7 NKJV)**

The more I immersed myself in listening to and singing Christian worship songs and hymns, the stronger my sense of connection with God became. I felt His presence tangibly, especially during our conversations. It was as if He was right there in the room with me. The Bible reassures us that His Spirit is always with us and that He never abandons us.

But here's the thing: understanding the goodness of the Lord comes from experiencing it first-hand. This is something I've personally witnessed. I've encountered many Christians, but it's unfortunate that some don't truly know the Jesus of the Bible or understand the significance of His finished work on the cross. To me, it seems like they use the Bible for personal gain, but I've always been careful not to do that. I embraced this faith to seek truth, regardless of the cost. All I ever desired was to discover if God truly existed. I didn't want to rely on others' words; I wanted to experience His presence myself. I longed to see how the Bible could transform us. While I've heard many testimonies of healing and deliverance, a part of me always wanted to experience it myself to fully believe.

God never disappointed me, though. I was asked to apply His principles in my life, and it worked wonders for me. That's all it took for me to have testimony after testimony of God's grace and goodness. It was almost like the universe waited for me to take a step in the right direction, and as soon as I did that, His Spirit revealed itself to me.

However, my journey to the new faith wasn't without its challenges. There were many things I had to take care of, like mending relationships within my family. I learned there was no point in responding to anger and hurt with the same reaction. Instead, I realised it's important to approach those situations with empathy since such emotions only step from deeper issues. Instead of reacting aggressively or getting offended, I began giving people space to calm down and think rationally. Now, what did it achieve? It prevented confrontations and arguments and helped diffuse the tension. Soon, I realised not only did it help calm me down, but they were also becoming calmer.

The best part is it wasn't only my salvation that made me firmly believe in God. It was also the way He transformed my husband's life. Indeed, God has a plan for everything, and my marriage was also a part of this big plan He had for me. While I was never able to truly understand my husband, I knew he had had issues in childhood.

He was only a lost boy trying to figure life out. At that point in life, I could either leave him or choose to stand by him. I decided to do the latter. I knew what it was going to cost me. My personal pleasure. But it wasn't like I had been living for my pleasure all along, so making this sacrifice for my husband seemed like a fair price to pay. And so, a new chapter in my life began, and I started guiding my husband towards the right path. A path to becoming a better human. A better husband. A better father to our children.

I'd be lying if I said there weren't times I wanted to give up. But I decided to keep going, even though it wasn't easy. I remember when he ended up in a hospital because of excessive drinking and self-harming. Yes, he hurt himself. It was so bad that he was put on a ventilator as he couldn't breathe for himself anymore. We waited for two whole days for any improvement in his condition, but there was none.

Finally, the doctors decided it was best to let him go and turn off the ventilator. I was asked to inform my family members about this tragedy. Can you even imagine that? As a wife, nothing could tear me apart more than the thought of losing my husband forever just when I thought my life was getting on the right track.

Yet, I didn't want to complain. To vent. To rant about my helplessness. I trusted God and his plan. The church I was attending back then showered us with lots of support. In fact, many of the members would accompany me to the hospital to pray for my husband.

Deep down in my heart, I knew God would help me. He wouldn't take my husband away, not yet, not so soon. I tuned into an Asian Indian radio channel where I rang the lady to pray for my husband. What started as a desperate attempt to get God to hear my prayers turned into many voices of listeners coming into agreement with my prayer. It was a beautiful moment, one that I still remember. It filled our lounge with a tangible presence, and I knew something miraculous was about to happen.

Something in me urged me to ring the hospital. As I did so, I was informed that my husband was breathing again – without the ventilator. Oh, I can't even begin to explain the relief I felt. God didn't abandon me. He listened to me. He was there for me, just like He promised he would.

Once my husband recovered, we started visiting a church together. One day after the end of the service, there was a call at the altar for salvation. Much to my surprise, my husband raised his hand, went up to the altar, and invited Jesus to be His Lord and Saviour. Even though I wanted this to happen, I did not know it would be so soon.

As for his spiritual journey, it was quite different from mine. Over time, I could see noticeable changes in him, even if they came slowly and gradually. I wasn't expecting an overnight change anyway. How could I? He had a long way to go from dealing with his alcohol addiction and unlearning wrong behaviour traits. I knew it was going to take a lot of time, and I had to be patient.

For quite some time, we also struggled with his controlling nature. For instance, whenever he would get in the car with me, he would try to control the way I drive. He used to tell me when to slow down or speed up and even turn my indicator on when I was turning the car. It was frustrating, to say the least. Yet, a part of me was ready to face such behaviour because I knew he couldn't just unlearn all his bad habits. He needed time, something I was ready to give him.

It didn't take me long to learn how to steer around this behaviour. One day, I sat him down and talked this driving issue out. I told him I'd drive him everywhere he wanted to go, but I needed him to stop interfering with my driving. And that was it. He listened to me, and we worked through it.

The day I graduated from Bible College was perhaps one of the best days for me. On our way back home, my husband mentioned his desire for water baptism. I couldn't believe my ears. Had I heard it right? Was he truly ready? It was the best thing he could have done for me on that particular day.

In the Bible, we learn a lot about reading and meditating to open our minds. That's exactly what we did. The material by Bible College helped us a lot, as new converts, to learn and grow in our faith. My husband, too, would listen to the founder of the Bible College, Andrew Wommack, on the CD player.

It brought wonderful changes to his personality. He was calmer, more patient, and more understanding. He even became more open to attending church with me whenever I wanted him to. He was turning into a good man, a man who was pleasant to be around. He started helping me around the house, and we began enjoying each other's company.

Our relationship blossomed as my husband and I developed a strong relationship with God himself. Things started to change for good, such as he started reducing his alcohol consumption. However, it wasn't easy. It was a long road to recovery. Besides, it wasn't just him this addiction affected. It was our entire family. We were still glad to have deliverance, though.

Looking back, I realise that God was with us the whole time. He had been there since the day we were born; it just took us a while to realise that we needed Him to guide us. The Bible says,

"But when He saw the multitudes, He was moved with compassion for them, because they were weary and scattered, like sheep having no shepherd." **(Matthew 9:36 NKJV)**

I remember when I first converted to Christianity. I felt so lost that I would pray, "Father God, I don't know what's best for me anymore. Please guide me to what is best for my life."

Even though it might seem unreal now, there comes a moment when God decides to intervene in our lives and enter our hearts. And when that happens, nothing and no one can take that away from us. The Bible also says,

"Ask, and it will be given to you; seek, and you will find; knock, and it will be opened to you. For everyone who asks receives, and he who seeks finds, and to him who knocks, it will be opened." **(Matthew 7:7-8 NKJV)**

Unless you've experienced this transformation yourself, you can't truly understand the truth this verse holds. It made my life easier, revealing the truth and helping me see through the lies of the world.

It wasn't until I started reading the Bible that I realised it's nourishment for the soul, healing and uplifting me in ways I can't fully explain. So, if you're reading this, my advice to you is: don't underestimate the words in the Bible.

It's not just a book; it's a holy scripture that teaches us how to live. It's a hidden treasure waiting to be discovered. No matter where you are or what you're going through, the Bible can guide you. I speak from personal experience.

This was just the beginning of a better life for me. It filled the emptiness in my heart and led me to live in the way of Jesus. It transformed me into the person I am today. The person you'll get to know better in the upcoming chapters of this book.

Chapter 9
Privacy & Personal Lives

"Let no corrupt word proceed out of your mouth, but what is good for necessary edification, that it may impart grace to the hearers."

Ephesians 4:29 NKJV

Let me tell you something, writing a book on your life isn't exactly a walk in the park. It takes you on a walk down memory lane, and this little stroll can sometimes bring back painful memories if we don't look at them with the right lens. Memories that we had decided to bury. Memories that used to haunt us for a long time.

And once I relived all those moments with the Holy Spirit, my guide and friend, I realised more healing of the heart was taking place. A lot more tears of healing needed to be shed. So, when I started working on this book, I was also faced with this decision: Should I name and shame those people?

But no. I do not want to do that. I never did. And that's not even why I began writing this book in the first place. This book is for telling people that there's always hope for betterment. Even the darkest days of our life fade away when the sun rises on a new day.

Besides, wouldn't it be contradictory of me to call them out when I say I now live my life according to the principles of the Bible? It teaches us to let go, set boundaries, and not get offended. The purpose of this book is not to embarrass or expose anyone. Instead, it is to motivate all those suffering out there. I shared my life experiences to prove how things work out when we put our faith in Jesus.

In a scripture, the Bible says,

"But God has chosen the foolish things of the world to put to shame the wise, and God has chosen the weak things of the world to put to shame the things which are mighty." **(I Corinthians 1:27 NKJV)**

If you ask me, I believe I was among these foolish people. It wasn't until God's spirit drew me to Himself and I made myself receptive to His Spirit that I truly put my faith in Him. Now that I think of it, I have done all kinds of sins to anger Jesus before I converted to Christianity. Did God ever punish me for things I did when I didn't know any better? No, He did not. In fact, He has been so kind to heal me when I turned to Him.

So, why should I seek revenge on those who wronged me when they may not have known any better either? It's a common feeling, but I've come to understand that revenge isn't important. It's more crucial to focus on repairing relationships, especially with those close to us. Without a strong connection to God, our Creator, worldly relationships can suffer. Looking back, I've also learned the value of privacy. For much of my life, I was open to everyone, but it only led to criticism and gossip. I've realised that keeping some aspects of our life private can protect our peace of mind. Not every relationship deserves to be at the centre of our life; we have the power to choose which ones matter most.

And while we are on this topic, let me share another snippet from the Bible:

"Repay no one evil for evil. Have regard for good things in the sight of all men. If it is possible, as much as it depends on you, live peaceably with all men. Beloved, do not avenge yourselves, but rather give place to wrath; for it is written, "Vengeance is Mine, I will repay," says the Lord. Therefore, "If your enemy is hungry, feed him; If he is thirsty, give him a drink; For in so doing, you will heap coals of fire on his head." Do not be overcome by evil but overcome evil with good." **(Romans 12:17-21 NKJV)**

Come to think of it, Lord Jesus is the perfect example of not repaying evil with evil. He didn't retaliate when he was insulted. He didn't threaten others for making him suffer. Instead, he simply left the matter to the One who judges justly. You can read about his entire life, and you'll not find a single instance in which he tried to get back at anyone. He taught us not to lash out and he himself used to practice what he preached.

Sometimes, when others are giving us a hard time, we feel challenged. But as someone who has gone through all of this, trust me, making them look bad won't make us feel good about ourselves. What really helps is talking the problem out with the one who has our best interest at heart – Jesus, our Lord and Saviour – and praying for them. It has worked for me, and it will work for you, too.

While my faith in Jesus has allowed me to sort out many of my relationships, there's still a long way to go. Many relationships are yet to be restored. But I'm hopeful. I know God is at work, and when the timing is right, even the tiniest pieces of my life will fall back into place.

Chapter 10
Supportive Circles

"And let us consider one another in order to stir up love and good works, not forsaking the assembling of ourselves together, as is the manner of some, but exhorting one another, and so much the more as you see the Day approaching."

Hebrews 10:24-25 NKJV

Ever wondered why wolves always travel in a pack? It's because there's strength in numbers. They become untouchable, protected by the unity of the group. Let's look at it with another lens. Imagine a single strand of spaghetti. It's easy to snap, right? But if you take the whole packet of spaghetti and try breaking it, you'll find it's much tougher to break. That's exactly what being in a group does for you. It makes you stronger, unbreakable, and shielded from external blows.

I've been navigating life's challenges all alone until the Holy Spirit saved me. And once I landed on the right path, I never found myself alone. The teachings of the Bible constantly promote fellowship among believers. For instance, in John 1:7, the Bible says:

"But if we walk in the light, as he is in the light, we have fellowship with one another, and the blood of Jesus his Son cleanses us from all sin."

This underscores that once you walk in the light, you share the transformative power of Christ's blood with the other believers – making you one of them. In Act 2:42, we learn that Christianity is not only about devoting yourself to the teachings of the Holy Scripture. Rather, it also involves seeking fellowship, breaking bread, and prayer.

The believers ought to be united to ultimately maintain the unity of the Holy Spirit, as stressed in Ephesians 4:3. Being like-minded with fellow Christians allows us to be more at peace and content with life.

I never got to experience the true meaning of unity until I accepted Jesus as my Lord and Saviour. I only understood what support and joy truly looked like when I enrolled in the three-and-a-half-year-long Bible College course. Being fortunate enough to forge genuine, kind friendships at the college, I found myself surrounded by people oozing with love.

I had left everything behind to join the college. You might remember how I mentioned quitting my job for it. Back then, I had no idea how things would work out for me and our home. However, the Lord works in mysterious ways.

Owning a four-bedroom house, we used to have ample space in our home, considering how it was just me, my husband, and our son living there. So, we decided to rent out the unoccupied rooms to students who came from abroad. This arrangement worked pretty well for all of us. The students got a nice place to stay while they completed their studies, and I paid my tuition fees from their rent money.

I was also able to make wonderful connections with people from all walks of life during my time at the Bible College. Perhaps it was due to our diverse past and the challenges we all had to endure up until our paths crossed at the college that made us understand each other so well. We could easily open up to one another, becoming a source of encouragement for each other. Most of all, it was our faith in Jesus Christ that kept us connected.

In the second year of the college program, we were supposed to participate in a mission trip across the world. Even though I wanted to visit India, somehow, it wasn't possible at that time, and I was chosen to go to Bulgaria with six other people.

Considering it was my first time on such a mission, I was naturally nervous to preach God's message in jam-packed Churches. But I couldn't believe the love and attention I received during my time there. Due to my skin tone, the people of Bulgaria felt a sense of familiarity with me, and they listened to me with an open heart and wanted to learn about my life journey thus far.

I met Chance and Dee Dee on this trip to Bulgaria. They were a precious couple who believed that the heart of ministry is believing in people when they don't believe in themselves. They were firm believers in the fact that God has gifted everyone with some potential, and they must fulfil their purpose in this world.

Chance and Dee Dee had an interesting background, too. They had been dedicated to ministry since they first got married. After coming to know God, they felt compelled to share their transformative, life-changing experiences with others. Their passion has always been to help those who are hurting and in need of a second chance.

In 2008, they went on their first short-term mission trip to Greece, spending just a day or two in Bulgaria with a church in a Roma village. Upon returning home, they felt a strong desire to return and spend more time in Bulgaria. The following year, in 2009, they brought their 14-year-old son for a mission trip focused entirely on Bulgaria, working with teenagers in another Roma community. It became clear to all three of them that they would one day return to Bulgaria permanently.

They began the process of moving their family to Bulgaria with much prayer, fundraising, quitting their jobs, selling their home, and completing loads of paperwork. On November 2, 2011, they left

America with only a suitcase each and flew to Bulgaria to begin their new adventure.

It wasn't until 2013 that my paths crossed with them in Bulgaria during my first mission trip. I felt a strong spiritual connection to them almost instantly. After returning from this life-changing experience and forming bonds with the people there, I was inspired to continue visiting and sharing my life journey and God's love with them. Bulgaria is like a second home for me now.

As for Chance and Dee Dee, I'm still in touch with them, and we occasionally meet up when they are in the UK. Like them, I made quite a few friends at the Charis Bible College that I'm in contact with to this day. We all form a supportive network of believers and friends who stand by each other through thick and thin.

Walking through this path hasn't exactly been easy, but Jesus has always been there for me. In one way or another, I'm always reassured of His goodness ever since I have come to faith. Back in my second year at college, I was short of £1500 for my final term fees. Feeling anxious, I went to the Director's office to discuss my situation. To my astonishment, he informed me that my fees had already been covered. I was overwhelmed with gratitude and curiosity, but I never discovered who my generous benefactor was.

Something similar happened in my third year as well. My car was written off due to an accident I was involved in, leaving me without a vehicle. During this time, a couple studying at the college approached me and mentioned that their son had just bought a new car and I could have his old one. I asked how much they wanted for it, but they said they didn't want anything and simply wished to bless me with it. Remarkably, a friend and I had been praying about my situation, and she had told me that a car was on its way and that it would be red. Indeed, the car I was blessed with was red.

But these stories don't end here. I remember someone once handed me a booklet about the Promised Land, where Jesus Christ was born and walked in Israel. This was when I was new to my faith, and ever since then, I've had a deep desire to walk in that sacred place.

Unexpectedly, another friend from the Bible College called me in 2017 and mentioned her plans to go there along with her Church group. She asked if I'd be willing to join them, and I laughed it off, considering I didn't have enough finances.

A few days later, she called again, telling me that she had paid all my expenses and that I should start packing. It was like a dream come true for me. I couldn't believe that God had presented me with this wonderful opportunity. Had it not been for Him, I would've never imagined stepping foot on that land.

I am eternally grateful for that friend and all the others I met during my time at Charis Bible College. I also deeply admire Andrew and Jamie Wommack, the founders of the college. What they have set out to do isn't easy, but with each passing day, they make a difference in someone's life and in the entire world by bringing people like me closer to God, empowering us, and educating us. I knew in my heart that I was ready for whatever God had willed for my life once I had completed the three-year program.

When Covid'19 pandemic struck the world, and we were all locked indoors, I decided to share my faith and devotional thoughts online. It was merely something to keep myself occupied during the lockdown, and I had no idea what it would lead to. Little did I know it would grow tremendously over the years, enabling me to empower people to change their perspective and grow in their identity in Christ.

Now that I look back, I realise none of it would have been possible without prayer and God's word. The Holy Spirit sent me a word to teach and empower people. He even put it in my heart that I had a ministry which I should call Holy Word Empowered Ministries.

Today, I individually lead three groups of followers in English, Punjabi, and Urdu language. I translate my devotionals into these languages using Google Translate so that more and more people can learn and understand the teachings of the Bible and grow in their faith in Jesus Christ, our Lord and Saviour.

What started out as sort of a leisure activity has transformed into something much bigger. We hold virtual meetings on Zoom and WhatsApp from Monday to Friday, where we encourage, teach, and support our growing community.

It's a sanctuary for people like me—those who have faced life's challenges for so long and have finally found the right path. It's for those who are seeking to transform their lives under the guidance of the Holy Spirit. I've come to learn that Jesus never leaves us alone, and it's my vision to ensure these people feel the same way.

Chapter 11
Living A Victorious Life

"Blessed is the man Who walks not in the counsel of the ungodly, Nor stands in the path of sinners, Nor sits in the seat of the scornful, But his delight is in the law of the Lord, And in His law he meditates day and night. He shall be like a tree Planted by the rivers of water, That brings forth its fruit in its season, Whose leaf also shall not wither; And whatever he does shall prosper. The ungodly are not so But are like the chaff which the wind drives away. Therefore the ungodly shall not stand in the judgment, Nor sinners in the congregation of the righteous. For the Lord knows the way of the righteous, But the way of the ungodly shall perish."

Psalms 1:1-6 NKJV

One thing about life is that it's unpredictable. The story behind how someone got to where they are today is often hidden. But I wanted to narrate the story of my life to the world because not all of us have the courage or the means to turn our lives around.

Like me, there are tons of women stuck in the same patterns of generational trauma, societal stereotypes, and enduring abuse. I have laid out my life story over the last ten chapters, revealing how far I have come since breaking free from the shackles of abuse. It hasn't been easy, to say the least. But was it worth it? Every single second.

Unfortunately, a guide on transforming your life doesn't exist since everyone's circumstances vary from situation to situation. But what I have found helpful is having a perspective. A positive one. If you keep viewing your life through the lens of misery, you'll never gather the courage to make things better for yourself. Living a victorious life entails viewing it with optimism and believing that there's definitely light at the end of the tunnel.

Most of all, it's important to realise that life isn't just a constant uphill climb. At different stages, we all face challenges and encounter experiences we wish we could have avoided. In such times, it helps to have faith in a higher source. But there's a pitfall to it – not everyone recognises Jesus Christ as their true Lord and Saviour.

Some people are deceived by their beliefs, and they fall for any of the man-made faiths on Earth. Granted, it might temporarily soothe the conscience and bring hope and comfort, but it only takes a few to recognise that all of this is nothing but deception.

We are conditioned in a way to accept the beliefs of our ancestors without question. Being curious is frowned upon when it comes to matters related to faith. However, for someone like me, it was important not to follow the generational footsteps of others but to question the existence of God. And why wouldn't I? Considering my encounters with adversity time and time again, I couldn't help but wonder if God truly existed. And if He did, why was He allowing so much suffering to come into my life?

In the Bible, God says:

"For by grace you have been saved through faith, and that not of yourselves; it is the gift of God, not of works, lest anyone should boast." **(Ephesians 2:8-9 NKJV)**

It wasn't until I familiarised myself with the teachings of the Bible that I understood the true meaning behind these verses. These words clearly state that our salvation isn't something we can earn by our own efforts. Rather, it's a gift given freely by God because of His love for us.

Isn't it simply amazing? When we acknowledge God as our Creator and understand His role in our lives, it brings us wisdom and clarity about why we're here on Earth. It helps us see that life is about understanding our purpose in the Lord's bigger plan and living in a way that honours Him. This understanding filled me with a sense of direction and fulfilment because it taught me that I am loved and valued by the Creator of the universe.

It's easy to say you believe in something. However, being a true believer as per the New Testament goes beyond simply acknowledging Jesus as the Messiah. It encompasses loyalty and faithfulness to Him. It is more than merely learning about the teachings of the Bible and regarding them as the truth. You should let that information change your way of life.

Only once you become a believer and let the truth of Jesus Christ imbed in your heart can your life be truly transformed. This transformation makes an entirely new creation, and it's way more than intellectuality; it's a profound internal change that involves turning away from old ways and fully committing to Christ.

The Bible also refers to believers as disciples – people who seek to mirror the character of their role models. Because of their commitment to imitating Jesus, detractors mockingly dubbed the disciples of Jesus "little Christs" or "Christians."

Even though the disbelievers meant for this term to be an insult, they didn't realise it was the best compliment a believer could receive. Indeed, our goal as believers is to be "little Christs" in everything that we do, from our words to our actions and values.

In Scripture, there's a clear distinction between those who follow Christ and those who don't. The term "unbeliever" refers to those who oppose Christian beliefs and values. In 2 Corinthians 6:14–15, Paul advises believers not to form close ties with unbelievers because righteousness and lawlessness, light and darkness, and Christ and Belial (a term for wickedness) have nothing in common. Believers are seen as being transformed more and more into the likeness of Jesus, making their differences from unbelievers even clearer as they grow in their faith journey.

When Scripture compares those who believe in Christ with those who don't, it highlights significant lifestyle differences. Believers are known for their love, their pursuit of holiness, and their desire to reflect Christ's character. The Bible teaches that true believers cannot continue in lifestyles that defy God's standards, as their salvation brings a new nature. Just as a fish can't survive out of water, born-again hearts can't thrive in sin because of their new spiritual life.

Those who belong to Christ don't persist in sinning. Likewise, those who live in sin are not God's children but are influenced by the devil. Jesus came to earth to undo the devil's work, and those born of God cannot persist in sin because they are transformed by God's presence within them.

Hebrews 11:6 emphasises that faith is essential to please God, and without it, unbelievers remain spiritually dead in their sins. The consequences of sin, which include God's wrath, can only be overcome through reconciliation with God through Christ. Faith in Jesus Christ is the key difference between those who please God and those who do not.

Jesus Himself taught in Matthew 5:45 that God's blessings extend to everyone, regardless of their spiritual state. This includes both the righteous and the unrighteous, reflecting God's fairness and universal care.

In the Bible, discipline means more than just punishment; it's about moral training, guidance, and correction that help us grow spiritually, develop our character, and mature as Christians. In order to live a fulfilling and successful life, the book of Proverbs emphasises accepting discipline with humility.

If you look around, you'll realise we all discipline ourselves in various ways. Be it starting a new job or training for races like athletes do, discipline instils focus in us, enabling us to overcome challenges and achieve our goals.

However, considering the dynamic nature of the world today, it's easy to get caught up in the daily grind. Amidst this, we often lose track of our true purpose in life – the worship and love of God. The Bible instructs us to run our race with our eyes fixated on Christ:

"Let us run with perseverance the race marked out for us, fixing our eyes on Jesus, the pioneer and perfecter of faith" **(Hebrews 12:1-2)**

To focus means to give your full attention to something. When we focus on Christ, we're giving Him our undivided attention. We're thinking about Him and His teachings, keeping Him at the centre of our thoughts. This makes perfect sense because Jesus is the leader of the church, the first to rise from the dead, and should be supreme in everything. It's only right that He becomes the main focus of our lives.

Naturally, as humans, we tend to sometimes deviate from the right path. However, what truly counts is acknowledging our mistakes and turning back to God. Repenting for our sins is a great way to invite change, restoration, and peace in our lives.

Consistency is the key here. Fortunately, the Bible contains ample information to help us stay focused on Christ. The following verses from Colossians are merely an example of the help you can find from the Holy Scripture:

"Since then, you have been raised with Christ, set your hearts on things above, where Christ is, seated at the right hand of God. Set your minds on things above, not on earthly things. For you died, and your life is now hidden with Christ in God. When Christ, who is your life, appears, then you also will appear with him in glory." We are to focus on "things above," remembering that Christ is seated in the place of glory and power. The reason for the command is also given: because we have been raised to new life with Christ. To focus on the things above, we must consciously remove our focus from "earthly things", and the reason is given: we have died to self, and Christ is our very life. Helping us stay focused on Christ is the reminder that Jesus is coming again, and when we see Him we will know glory." **(Colossians 3:1-4)**

As a new believer, I struggled with understanding what consistency in the Christian life looked like in the day-to-day application and how I could achieve it. Then, I discovered that Jesus had already shown us the way in His Sermon on the Mount.

A steady walk of faith springs from a deep love for God. We give our whole selves to Him and make His kingdom our top priority. We pour our time, talents, and energy into preparing for eternity, where our true reward lies. We regularly gather with other believers for encouragement and devote ourselves to the Bible, fellowship, and prayer.

A consistent believer knows that life on earth, with all its ups and downs, is just temporary. Since every earthly prize and challenge will eventually fade, we focus on the unchanging promises of heaven and strive to live holy and godly lives.

The Bible often celebrates persistence as a positive trait, linking it to endurance and perseverance. The Bible even highlighted this in a story about a widow who kept begging a judge for justice. She wouldn't take "no" for an answer, and eventually, the judge gave in. This story is a source of encouragement for us to be just as persistent in our prayers. When our goals are righteous, persistence is a powerful virtue.

Being persistent in prayer, faith, and doing good is always praised in the Bible because the motives are pure. However, persistence turns negative when it's driven by selfish motives. If we keep persisting in sin, other Christians are actually instructed to correct us. Continuing in a sinful lifestyle shows we haven't truly been transformed by the Holy Spirit.

For those who want to please God, persistence is what keeps us on track. It's about putting one foot in front of the other, no matter the temptations, doubts, or discouragements that come our way. Isaiah 40:31 promises that those who wait for the Lord will gain new strength, soar like eagles, run without getting tired, and walk without becoming weary. Waiting for the Lord means staying persistent in righteousness until He answers or delivers us.

How can believers avoid being conformed to the world? By transforming our minds. This transformation happens through the power of God's Word. We need to hear it, read it, study it, memorise it, and meditate on it. The Bible, guided by the Holy Spirit, is the only force on earth that can shift us from worldliness to true spirituality. It's all we need to be fully prepared for every good work. When we let God's Word shape us, we can discern His good, pleasing, and perfect will.

God's will for every believer is to live as a living sacrifice for Jesus Christ. This means applying the truth of our new identity in the Bible to our daily lives. It's about changing our perspective, harnessing our emotions, and living victoriously over every challenge we face.

At first, this might seem like a lot to take in. But you can always start small, just like I did. Take baby steps in the right direction, and you'll see your life turn around. Wonderful things will come your way, just as they did for me. My journey is far from over, but I'm confident that the Lord has amazing plans for me ahead.

The End

Printed in Great Britain
by Amazon

47297273R00059